RUNNING ON TIRED LEGS

BILL GRAHAM

CONTENTS

Title Page	1
Prologue	5
1 Born to Run	8
2 For the Love of Sport	15
3 The First Miles	21
4 1-Brockhole to Mardale	29
5 A World Away	33
6 Marathon Talk	39
7 Time for a Change	45
8 Marathon Comrades	51
9 2-Mardale Head to Howtown	57
10 One for the Road	61
11 Nowhere to Run	67
12 Peak Times	73
13 Walk Don't Run	79
14 3-Howtown to Patterdale	86
15 The End of an Era	90
16 Head for the Hills	95
17 A Step in the Right Direction	102
18 Climb Every Mountain	109
19 4-Patterdale to Dunmail	116

20	Running on Tired Legs	124
21	Stronger for Longer	132
22	Into the Hot Seat	138
23	A Day in the Lakes	146
24	5-Dunmail to Langdale	153
25	A Green Man	157
26	Too Tired to Run	163
27	A World of Running	169
28	6-Langdale to Brockhole	176

PROLOGUE

"Nothing, not even pain, lasts forever. If I can just keep putting one foot in front of the other, I will eventually get to the end."
-Kim Cowart

It's two days after my sixtieth birthday and I am standing nervously on the start line along with a hundred and twenty other athletes in the dark of a chilly Lake District morning. Lots of head torches are on, photos are being taken and last minute words of encouragement handed out. The Lakeland Trails 100K Ultra race was due to start at 6am and with fifteen minutes to go my head torch is still in my rucksack. I have decided that's where it will stay until I get much further into the race as I feel confident that it will be light enough to see within half an hour of the start. Until that point I will rely on the half-light and other people's head torches. The head torch I am carrying is very minimalistic but at this time that does not concern me too much because I am not too sure that I will get beyond half way or, if I do have a successful run, I will only need a head torch for the last hour or so. For now my only thought is for the 100km of Lakeland trails that await me over the coming hours.

I have the usual pre-race nerves and probably more so for this event because of two reasons. Firstly this will be the furthest I have ever run in my life and secondly my preparation has been far from ideal. Just a few weeks earlier I was seriously thinking of dropping down to the 50k event because of the lack of training miles. My good friend Bryan, who was probably the most mentally strong person I had ever run with, spoke to me and said he felt the lack of preparation and the fact that he could not get his head round the distance meant he was not ready to take on the challenge. At that point I had serious doubts about my ability to complete the course, so I decided to test myself over a familiar off road route around my home town of Bristol. It did not go particularly well even though I managed twenty eight miles. I struggled throughout and even stopped for a cup of tea and some nutrition at eighteen miles. My legs felt like lead, my knees were sore and the current foot injury I was carrying, Mortons Neuroma, was giving me a lot of pain. Should I really be doing this sort of thing at my age with a history of dodgy knees and foot problems, probably not, but there was something about this sort of challenge that I could not resist.

I had come to love this area of the UK and had spent many hours walking, biking and running in these mountains. This came about many years earlier when I had picked up a long term running injury and started walking as an alternative. A few years ago my sister had asked me if there was one place in world I could live then where would it be. I did not hesitate and said the Lake District. The Lake District has a beauty that exists nowhere else and part of that beauty is that it is all accessible. There are taller mountain ranges, there are mountain ranges that cover vast areas but there is something special about the Lake District and until you have been there it is quite difficult to explain what that special something is. If you were standing right in the middle of the Lake District you could choose to go anywhere else in the National Park and you would be there within an hour. I have been to the Scottish Highlands, the Alps, the Pyrenees, the Rockies, the Drakensburg in South Africa and the mountains of New Zealand but give me the Lake District every time.

The half-way point of the Lakeland Trails 100K Ultra was the start of the 50k event and my wife Claire was taking on that challenge. The perfect run would see me reaching her start not too long after she had set off. Then I would steadily close the gap on her and maybe we would even run the last few miles together. I did not think that it would pan out this way because I could not really see myself getting beyond the mini buses at half way, but despite the negativity somewhere in the back of my mind there was a little voice saying "you can do it". Running had been a big part of my life for many years and had helped in my development both physically and mentally. I was no longer as fast or as fit as I used to be, but that was no reason for me to give up. While I was still able to, I would continue to take on this sort of challenge. I had spent a few years running longer distances and felt I knew how to tackle these mammoth events. So where did this steely determination to 'give it a go' come from? What was it that made me think that, despite the lack of ideal preparation, an aging body and a foot injury, I could cope with 100km of tough, demanding Lakeland mountain terrain? This is the story of that event along with my reflection on nearly forty years of running, the highs, the lows, the successes, the failures, the injuries, the doubts and finally the aching feeling in my legs that had been there since my first marathon back in 1981.

1   BORN TO RUN

"My doctor told me that jogging could add years to my life. I think he was right. I feel ten years older already."
-Milton Berle

I was born in Liverpool at Mill Road Hospital on 12 September 1953 and have only vague recollections of those early years. I was the second child of Albert and Teresa, the first being my brother Allen, who was 18 months my senior. My sister Pam was the next addition in April 1957 followed by a real late comer, Vicky in 1971. My parents told me I was a sickly child and spent most of the first six months of my life in hospital with various ailments including a long bout of pneumonia, which at the time had quite a high fatality rate. Later in life I was to suffer chest problems which probably relate back to that early illness.

The house where we lived in Keble Street was a modest three bedroom terraced property, which we shared with my Gran and my mum's sister Jean. There was an outside toilet at the end of the yard and an old tin bath hanging by a nail on the wall just outside the back door. I remember my Dad saving me the journey to the loo in the winter by getting me to stand by the back door and telling me to pee in the yard. Sounds awful, but it was certainly better than making that dark journey to the outside loo. It was a cold and dismal place where spiders were in abundance and an electric light was just a fantasy.

What else do I remember of those early years, well I know I was accident prone and was forever falling and banging my head. The two worst episodes of this resulted in visits to hospital after first tripping over and cracking my forehead on a brick wall. While on the second occasion I was playing in the park when I was struck by a wayward half brick. The other memories were of the house and the street we lived in.

The house always seemed to be dark and cold and I can remember being a bit scared of going upstairs on my own. I think this was mainly due to the fact that there was no light on the stairs, and until you got into the bedroom, it was dark. I used to lie in bed and listen to, what seemed to be, babies crying in the dark. This was very scary and could not understand why babies would be out so late at night. It wasn't until years later that I discovered it was cats making these strange, baby like, noises. We had two rooms downstairs, the kitchen/dining area and the 'parlour'. The parlour was a room that you were never allowed into unless you were invited. It usually contained a couple of armchairs and a display cabinet with lots of little ornaments. It was always kept spotlessly clean and I can even remember being in there with Mum one day as she religiously polished all the brass ornaments. This room was for special guests like the priest or the rent man so we spent most of our time in the kitchen/dining area. This room became the bathroom every Friday when the old tin bath would be dragged in and filled with hot water that was boiled in pans on the cooker. The children usually got in the water first then the adults, this meant we had the warmer and cleaner water. In the winter the house was very cold, one coal fire was lit in the kitchen/dining area making this toasty warm while the rest of the rooms were like refrigerators.

The street was very much like 'Coronation Street'. It was not very long and the front doors came out on to the road. There was a pub at one end and at the other there was a corner shop. Occasionally we would be given a penny to spend and we would rush off to the corner shop to see what delights it held. Our playground was the streets we lived in and some of those streets were only half lived in, with the other half being the remains of houses that had been bombed during the war. These house remains were a source of great intrigue to us kids so they became part of our playground. Wandering through these remains was exciting, but rather dangerous and if my memory serves me right they eventually fenced these areas off because of the risks associated with half demolished homes. We did embark on occasional trips to the local Kensington Park, an area that seemed huge to me at the time. It was also a bit scary as a lot of bigger kids were there and the usual amount of bullying took place. The streets of Liverpool were not a place for the faint hearted but as I was still very young it did not seem to affect me too much. I do remember the occasion I received the wayward half brick. We were in Kensington Park and were having a stone throwing fight with another gang. All pretty harmless until one of theirs decided the stones were too small and launched the half brick in our direction.

Just round the corner, on Marvin Street, lived my auntie Margaret and Uncle George with their children. My dad and George were brothers and my Mum and Margaret were sisters so we were always a bit more than just cousins and we never seemed to live too far away from each other. Wherever Marg and George went we seemed to follow shortly after. Dad and George even worked together at, what was then, the De Havilland factory in Broughton near Chester. Today this site is Airbus owned and manufactures the wings for all the different variants of Airbus aircraft.

When I was 6 years old we left Liverpool to take up residence In Brentwood Road, Blacon, Chester. The move took us closer to Marg and George, who had moved to Blacon a few months earlier, and it made it easier for Dad to get to work. Compared to where we lived in Liverpool the three bedroom council house we occupied was quite luxurious. We had an inside toilet and a bathroom, as well a small rear garden.

By this age I was a very vulnerable character. I was a painfully shy individual and did not take criticism easily. I had a slight stammer and being ginger and freckled with sticky out ears, would blush at the drop of a hat. If a girl spoke to me I would just freeze, no words would come out and I would just stand there feeling the colour come in to my cheeks until I felt I would explode.

I started school at St.Werburgh's Juniors, which was in the heart of Chester just a few yards from the Cathedral and the city walls. It was at St. Werburgh's that I was to take part in my first athletic event and also played in my first football matches.

The school football team trained and played in the centre of Chester race course (The Roodee) next to the river Dee. They weren't the best pitches in the world, in fact for most of the year they seemed to be under water. When they became too waterlogged matches were cancelled but training was moved along the river to an area called the meadows. Now the Roodee pitches weren't great but compared to the meadows they were like Wembley. The meadows were an area where sheep and cattle were grazed and the grass was left uncut for this purpose. This meant that if the livestock were grazing we would have to clear an area to train on which was consequently covered in fresh manure. If the livestock weren't grazing then we had to train on grass which came up to our knees.

We weren't the best team around and there weren't many local teams that we ever managed to beat. Most weeks we received a sound thrashing and I was to meet up with some of the better players from these opposing teams when I moved on to secondary school.

In my last year at St. Werburgh's the school entered a team in a local Athletics Meeting and announced there would be trials in the coming week. I was desperate to get a place in the team and could hardly sleep the night before the trials.

The trials took place in the school yard as we did not have a playing field. This consisted of groups of children running aimlessly up and down the yard. With a background of playing football for the school team I felt this would stand me in good stead for the trials. As selections were made for each event without my name being mentioned, I felt downhearted and was about to give up on getting a place in the team, when they decided to do a trial for the hurdles. This trial was based on your ability to get yourself over a cane, which was balanced between two chairs, without falling over. It was hardly a major task as the chairs were junior size so the cane was only about twelve inches off the ground. I managed to do this on half a dozen occasions and this feat meant I was selected for this event. I was so excited I could have burst and could not wait to get home to tell Mum and Dad of this huge achievement. It was just a week before the event would take place and I rushed home informing my parents that I would require new athletics kit (white pumps, white shorts and white vest) as I had been selected to represent my school in the fifty yard hurdle event. Pumps were plimsolls, or as I now live in Bristol, daps. They were the kind that were made of canvas and were either lace up or elasticated. The soles were rubber and about the thickness of a bicycle tyre. No socks were worn with them and how I managed to run in these things I will never know, but I did and continued to do so right up until I left school.

With just a week to go there was no time for training and after a few days I had my kit except the vest. I only had string vests so it was off to see Auntie Margaret to see if I could borrow one. The only one she had that fitted belonged to my cousin Sue, so my first outing as an athlete was to be in a girls vest. I accepted the vest and made my way home to prepare for the big day.

A week passed and I don't think I have ever been so nervous about anything in my life. We arrived at the venue and I watched as the hurdles were placed over the fifty yard distance and was wondering why they were so high. This was nothing like the cane precariously balanced on the chairs in the school yard. This was more like a high jump event. The first few hurdle races took place and it seemed that at least one person in every race ended up being carried away sobbing after clattering a hurdle and hitting the ground. I was no longer nervous, I was petrified.

Mine was one of the last hurdle races, but finally my time came and one of the teachers gave me a few words of encouragement before sending me off to the start line. My mouth had dried up completely and I just wanted the race to start so I could get it over with. The gun went and we were off. This was my moment, my chance of glory, but it all came tumbling down, as

I did, when I hit the first hurdle and went crashing to the ground. As I hit the ground I just wanted it to swallow me up. I was embarrassed and thought it would be best to stay down and pretend I was hurt, but the only thing that was hurt was my pride and for some unknown reason I picked myself up and chased after the rest of the field. You may think that this tale ends with me gradually making my way through the field and gaining a glorious victory. Unfortunately this was not the case and I finished well and truly last. I was absolutely devastated and just burst into tears.

As I made my way back to my school mates feeling embarrassed and unable to control the tears a teacher from another school stopped me and said 'well done young man, of all the fallers in the hurdle races you were the only one who got up and carried on running. You may have come last but you showed guts and determination, be proud of what you have done'. Did this make me feel any better? Absolutely not, I re-joined my school mates and received lots of 'hard luck' comments, but inside I was hurting. My fragile confidence had been shattered. How was I to face my family after finishing last in my first ever race. Mum and Dad were very sympathetic and told me not to worry about it, there would be plenty more opportunities for me to compete, but my character just made me want to hide myself away feeling I had let the school down by coming last. Looking back now I see how it was just one race and I still had my football where I was performing well. The problem was I felt I needed to be successful to be liked. I was just a ginger haired, freckled character with a stammer and I was having trouble seeing myself as anything else. This lack of belief was like a huge weight around my neck. Some people need harsh words and a rollicking to perform at their best, I just needed an arm around my shoulder and to be told that I was good enough. There were times at that age when I really did feel alone, I was not mature enough to put into words how I was feeling and I know if I had spoken to my family about it they would have given me all the support I needed, but I did not even have the confidence to talk to them about the way

I felt.

As I have said sport was to play a big part in my development both physically and mentally. I was desperate to do well because I felt that success in this area would give me some self-esteem. Although my first love was football I did enjoy the hurdle race, even if it was not the best start to my athletic future, and was keen to do more. My move to secondary school helped me nurture my love of football but it was also where my athletic ability blossomed and my competitive spirit really came to the fore.

2 FOR THE LOVE OF SPORT

"If I am still standing at the end of the race, hit me with a board and knock me down, because that means I didn't run hard enough"
-Steve Jones

Overleigh Secondary Modern was the school I moved on to from juniors and the sporting acumen I gained was entirely down to the teachers, who were all very keen and encouraged everyone to take part in all forms of sport. In particular the teacher who stayed with us in sport through each year, Geoff Reynolds, was a huge influence. His drive, determination and coaching produced, what I believe, was one of the school's finest football teams. He was a hard man but very fair and it was a privilege to meet him again many years later at a school reunion, by which time he had received an MBE for his contribution to local schools football. He is now a life member and the President of Chester Schools Football Association.

There was a particular emphasis on football and when we gathered in the school yard for football trials I saw the familiar faces of the players who had given our team such a torrid time at junior level. Alan Morris, Dave Wilcocks, Micky Worrall and Nigel 'Gola' Clutton lined up alongside myself & John Relish who had played alongside me at St Werburgh's. I looked around me and all my insecurities washed over me. There was no way I was ever going to get into this football team when most of the players had more ability than I would ever have. Trials were held over the next couple of weeks and much to my surprise I was selected and went on play central defence for a while before moving to right back, and even managed to hold onto that position in the team. This was a very different team to the one I played in at junior school. We became quite a force to be reckoned with and were only beaten once in three years from 1965 to 1968. Most of the team also went on to represent Chester Schoolboys (myself included) and a few even went on to play for Cheshire County Boys. There were some very talented players amongst that group but only 3 ever went on to play professionally, and only one, John Relish, would make a career of it.

John and I lived close to each other in Blacon and spent quite a lot of time together as youngsters. John started his professional career with Chester before moving on to Newport County where he spent the rest of his career, as well as becoming a manager after his playing career was over. He had two spells at Newport 1974 to 1987 (337 appearances) and 1989 to 1990 (10 appearances) He played in their epic European Cup Winners Cup quarter final tie against Carl Zeiss Jena in 1981. I had the pleasure of being in the crowd for the home leg of that match. They had drawn 2-2 away so expectations were high for the return leg. Unfortunately they lost 1-0 at home despite giving the opposition a battering for most of the game. John played in defence and it was a bit unreal listening to the people around me commenting on someone I had played alongside for quite a few years. He obviously had a bit of a reputation as a hard man, again this was a bit of a surprise as he certainly was not like that when I played alongside him.

One of the other very talented players in that group was Alan Morris. Alan was captain of our school team and played at county level. He never quite made it professionally but was with Chester from 1972 to 1975 (no appearances), Bangor City in 1983 and 1984 (28 appearances), before returning to Chester where he made his one and only league appearance as a substitute in 1984. Sadly Alan died in 1998 when he was stabbed in the heart in the early hours of New Year's Eve outside his home in Hoole, Chester, aged just forty four. His girlfriend at the time was charged and acquitted and since then his murder has gone unsolved.

The only other player to have made a professional appearance was Micky Worrall who lived just a few doors away from me in Blacon.

During my time at Overleigh sport became a big part of my life, not only was I selected for the school football team but I also ran x-country for the school, I was in the school athletics team and I took part in cricket, swimming and tennis. My time at Overleigh certainly helped my development as both an athlete and a person.

A lot of the sport was inter-house competition. I was in the Thebans, one of the weaker sporting houses. The other houses were Spartans, Corinthians and the Athenians. From what I can remember it was usually the Thebans last then Spartans, Athenians and Corinthians.

School athletics was different back then and in my first year (1965/66) as I was never blessed with great speed I plumped for the longest distance I was allowed to run, which was four hundred and forty yards (1 lap of an imperial track). I showed some promise in this event and was selected to run for the school in the Chester Schools Championships. This was my first real competitive event since my fifty yard hurdle fiasco in junior school. Once again I was very nervous leading up to the event and was drawn in the outside lane. When the gun went I bolted like a frightened rabbit and did not see another runner until the first and second placed athletes passed me coming off the final bend. I had finished in third place and was amazed and overjoyed by this success. I had buried the ghost of my last place finish in the hurdles and raced home to proudly present my certificate to my parents.

My sporting prowess meant I gained a lot of support from fellow house mates during individual events such as x-country and athletics. In the first year I came 3rd in the school x-country and was beaten by someone who I played in the football team with. He was blessed with lightning speed which saw him excel in football, where he played centre forward, athletics (100yds & 220yds), x-country and swimming. His name was Chris Houston and a nicer bloke you could not wish to meet. I did battle with Chris in many x-country races but it was some time before I managed to beat him. I think this was down to the fact that he started smoking early in his secondary school life and also he did not really like the longer distances. Luckily for me he was a sprinter so I never had to do battle with him on the athletics track. In that same school year I had cemented my position in the school football team as well as my exploits in x-country and on the running track. That first school year went by in a bit of a blur and by the end I was still as painfully insecure and as shy as when it had started. I always managed to do well in lessons and was generally in the top 10 in most subjects, finishing the year with a good report.

The second year at Overleigh (1966/67) saw me grow in confidence along with academic and sporting success. I seemed to have lost my stammer but was still very easily offended and still blushed at the drop of a hat. The school football team had a great year, on the athletics track I had moved up to the 880 yards and the mile, and I also managed to get a bit closer to Chris Houston in the school x-country (I finished in second place not too far behind him). I had really started to enjoy my running and during the athletics season I tried nearly everything but it was clear that the longer distance was my forte.

By the time the Chester Schools x-country championships came round I was beating Chris over this distance and there was high hopes in the school of having double champions because my brother Allen was running really well. I was the favourite to win the U13 event while Allen was thought to have a good chance in the U15 race. The races took place on 10 February 1967 at Salvatorian College, Christleton. I was running really well and felt quite confident going into the race. The other Overleigh lads kept telling me I could win and once the race started I was out front with four or five other Overleigh runners including Chris Houston, John Relish and Micky Worrall. As we came to the end of a hedgerow the marshal sent us off to the right through a ploughed field. After running for about two hundred yards we heard a shout of "hey you're going the wrong way" we looked round to see the marshal who had sent us into this field now yelling at us to say we had gone wrong. We could see other runners running on the other side of the hedgerow at the top of the field. Rather than back track we all ran to the top of the field and scaled a hedge to get back in the race. The first one to reach the hedgerow was John Relish and he leapt over the hedge only to land in a big pile of fresh manure. The rest of us managed to scale the hedge while avoiding the manure and we were back in the race although somewhat further back than a few minutes earlier. After cursing the official we set about making our way through the field, although I think John spent the rest of the race running on his own.

The other Overleigh lads encouraged me to give chase and get back to the leaders and as I started to work my way through the field I eventually caught site of the race leader. I tried to settle myself for one last push and felt confident I could catch him as we made our way along a canal tow path. We veered off the tow path over a bridge, turned a corner and suddenly there was the finish line. I did not realise we were so close and made a dash for the line but was too late to catch the winner. I finished second and Chris came in not far behind me in third. Once again I was devastated and knew I was capable of winning but felt cheated by the official, the school complained but the result stood.

My brother had no such problems in his race and finished in first place, so all in all it was a great result for the school. The next day a small article appeared in the Liverpool Echo with the heading "Graham brothers boost triumph" detailing how Overleigh had triumphed in the Chester Schools Championships thanks to a first place for Allen Graham in the U15 event while his younger brother Billy managed second place in the U13 race. There was no mention of the mess up in my event and I was still angry at having been denied a real shot at winning, but at the same time I was excited at having my name in such a big newspaper.

Back at school training continued in readiness for the forthcoming athletics season and it was during this time that I really enjoyed my training. I tried every conceivable discipline including Pole Vault and Long Jump. I even had another go at the dreaded hurdles but decided it was definitely not for me. Our star hurdler was Andy Bromley who also seemed to be the school heartthrob, his blond hair and good looks making him the envy of us all. Andy was also in our school football team squad and his best position was right back, the same as me. We became good friends even though we were both after the same place in the football team. As well as an excellent hurdler Andy was also a very good swimmer. The athletic season proved to be quite successful as I gained a second place in the U13 mile final at the Chester Schools Championships. All in all a great year but the third year was where my life changed quite dramatically and although I continued to improve athletically, other distractions meant I was to suffer academically.

3 THE FIRST MILES

"If you want to become the best runner you can be, start now. Don't spend the rest of your life wondering if you can do it."
-Priscilla Welch

My third year at Overleigh (1967/68) started without me knowing about the major upheaval that was about to occur in my life. It started as just another school year. The football team started well and I was still heavily involved in both x-country and athletics. On the track I was working hard at the one mile event and had high hopes of success, both in this and the forthcoming x-country season.

Unfortunately the x-country season took an unexpected turn when the country was hit by foot and mouth disease. This restricted us to training around the school field and although I finally managed to beat Chris Houston in the school championship it was hardly the best preparation for the forthcoming county championships. Despite this I felt in good shape and was really looking forward to testing myself against the best in Cheshire.

The usual nervousness was with me in the lead up to the race and for the first time I felt pressure on me to achieve. Both teachers and pupils believed I had a real chance of a top three finish, which would mean I would be the first pupil from the school to represent Cheshire County at x-country. With a rich sporting history this was the one sport where the school had not had a county representative and this needed rectifying.

Foot and mouth restrictions meant the race itself became a few laps around a park which had a big hill on each lap. I started the race well enough but the hill was my undoing. Our school field was very flat so all my preparation was on a flat grassy surface. I did manage to stay with the lead group but faded on the last lap to finish in seventh place. I had still qualified for the county, because the top eight made up the team, but I was bitterly disappointed with this result and felt I had let the school down. Looking back I realise that I had not really put myself out in preparing. I just did laps round the school field whereas I should have been out doing some hill work, even if it meant doing it on the road. My disappointment was tempered somewhat by making the county team but I still felt I had let everybody down as there were such high hopes for me.

At the next school assembly it was announced that the school had its first county representative at x-country and I received enthusiastic applause. After assembly there were lots of congratulations from fellow pupils and this was the confidence booster I needed. I was now determined to do well at the upcoming English Championships to be held at Trentham Park, Stoke-on-Trent.

This confidence issue was something I had suffered with for many years, and on many occasions this fragility would impede my level of performance. Even when my confidence was high it would only take one disparaging remark to send it crashing down again. I always felt others were better than me and on many occasions felt I was not good enough. Funnily enough this manifested itself more in football than any other sport. It was a problem I tried to conquer but it was a long time before I succeeded, and before I did it cost me in terms of my level of performance. In training I was fine, and while I was playing at a level I felt I could cope with I was good, but as soon as I went to a level that I knew was going to be difficult, my confidence buckled. I trained hard and played really well but come match day I sometimes had a complete confidence failure. At one point, when I was in my late teens and playing at a reasonably high level, I was selected to play for the first team, I dealt with this issue by drinking before matches to try and relax myself. This started with just a couple of beers but in the end I was having 4 or 5 pints before a game. This obviously ended with my performances deteriorating, and after six or seven games I was sent back down to the reserve team. The manager at the time must have wondered why someone who performed so well in training and with the reserves was unable to do the same in first team matches.

The English x-country Championships came round and as no one else from the school was taking part it was up to Dad to drive me there. Stoke was not too far away but I was used to being surrounded by school mates for all sporting activities. Because of his work Dad very rarely saw either Allen or myself taking part in any sport. I can only recall him attending one football match at the school and one Athletic meeting. This changed a few years later when he actually became the manager of a football team I played in, so he saw me perform every week.

The x-country event took place on 23rd March 1968 and the junior race was held over three miles. There were thirty six counties represented with eight runners from each county. The start line consisted of thirty six narrow boxes just wide enough for each team to stand in single file, with Cheshire drawn in box thirty four. We were placed in the box based on finishing position in the county championships, so I was number seven. Nerves were once again playing a big part in how I was feeling and I remember it being a very cold and windy March day.

The gun went and it was a few seconds before I was out of the box and running. The first few hundred yards were in a wide open field but this soon narrowed down and there was a lot jostling for position when it did. As I was at the back of our box I did not get a great start, but after the initial jostling I settled into the race. The most predominant thing for me was how quick everybody was. This was not like a school race where it would quickly sort itself out and I would find myself in with the front group. These were all top county runners and nobody wanted to give an inch. I soon found the pace very difficult and as we started climbing through some woods I was hurting like hell and lots of runners seemed to be going past me. After about half way I noticed people started to drop out and fall by the wayside, but still the pace did not let up and the pain increased. As more and more dropped out I could not help thinking maybe I should drop out as well. There would be no shame in it because so many had already bailed, but then we started a downhill section and I found myself starting to pass people. I gained momentum and started to really work hard and actually found myself enjoying the occasion. The final half mile or so was back on a grassy field where I gave it everything I had finally crossing the finish line where I collapsed, absolutely exhausted. I had no idea where I had come, I certainly was not in the top few but I had finished when so many others had not. When the results were displayed I found out I had finished fifty eighth but the real victory was that I was the second Cheshire boy home.

Back at school with confidence on a high, my efforts were announced in assembly and again I received a big round of applause. With the athletics season still to come I was feeling good about everything. The football team were unbeaten during the season and I had done very well in the x-country.

The athletics season arrived and again I was working hard at getting my performances over the mile to a level where I could compete against the best in the county. My brother was also running well and there was talk at one point of arranging a one mile race during our school athletics meeting which would pitch him against me. Unfortunately the day of the meeting was particularly wet and even though it was a cinder track, it was decided to abandon this venture. It's a shame really because I think it would have been a good race, I had become fiercely competitive and would have relished the challenge.

I won the one mile event at the Chester Schools Championships and was confident of my chances at the forthcoming County Championships. However, before that happened I was called into action for the school to run in the Chester Championships at U15 level, which was one year above my age group. The reason they asked me to run was that their top miler, Alan Parker, was ill and would not be able to start.

At this point the old confidence issue arose. How was I expected to do well against boys who were one year older than me? Our PE Teacher Mr Reynolds persuaded me to give it a go and said he would be there to support me. As my brother was also competing at U16 level, my parents had decided to come along. As we were all changing and the usual banter was taking place I felt completely out of my comfort zone because these weren't the people I was used to and I retreated into my shell feeling I was not good enough to be there.

The weather was not kind to us on this day and heavy rain made conditions very difficult plus the meeting was on a grass track. I did not own a pair of spikes although you could borrow school ones if you wanted. For some reason I had decided not to and was wearing my old white pumps. I remember going outside before my event and using my blazer to keep warm as I spoke with Mum and Dad. They gave me words of encouragement and told me to just do my best.

I got to the start line and looked around nervously at my fellow competitors. They all looked so much stronger and fitter than me. I know Alan Parker had been a hot favourite for this event and in his absence the lad from Bishop's School was now the one to beat. The track itself had a bit of a slope so on the first bend there was a little climb followed by a slight downhill on the next bend. It was still raining as the gun went and we were off. I quickly settled into the pack for the first lap and as no one made a move the whole field was still together at the end of the lap. The second lap started and I could see Mr Reynolds shouting at me to get closer to the front. I tried to work my way to the front of the pack but was still nervous about being there. By the end of the second lap I was lying about fourth and there was Mr Reynolds again, this time screaming at me to go out front. As I have already said, Mr Reynolds was a hard man, and when he told you to do something you did it. So at the beginning of lap three I bolted to the front and gave it everything I had. The Bishop's School athlete was at the front and he just let me go. So did the rest of the field. They did not know me so I was no threat. The track was becoming more and more slippery and as I started the final lap I was starting to doubt that I had the stamina to keep this up. The other Overleigh lads were screaming at me to keep going and Mr Reynolds was demanding even more, telling me to sprint for home. I did not dare look back and just put everything I had into that final lap, expecting that at any moment the rest of the field would come storming past me. I reached the final bend and could feel myself slipping on the slight slope, but I dare not slow down otherwise I knew I would be caught. I could also hear the Bishop's School supporters shouting their man on, so I knew he was not far behind me. Even in this position with just twenty or thirty yards to go I did not believe I could win. I just kept running and did not look behind until I had crossed the finish line, I was shattered, covered in mud and the Bishop's athlete was about five yards behind me, I had won! True to form, Mr Reynolds came up to congratulate me and then proceeded to tell me off for not getting to the front sooner.

To win was a great feeling and all those doubts and insecurities I had before the race just disappeared. Victory was sweet but I felt for the Bishop's athlete as I overheard some of their supporters informing him that he had been beaten by someone who was a year below him.

Back at school there were more congratulations and lots of support for the forthcoming County Championships. Preparation was going well and I was really beginning to like finishing in first place. I had been working hard and was growing more and more confident.

The County Championships took place at The Athletics Centre, Hartford in Nantwich on 15th June 1968. The weather was good but because of the number of athletes for the mile there would be two heats with the two winners plus the six fastest losers progressing to the final. My heat was at 12.15 and the final was scheduled for 5 o'clock, the second last event of the meeting. I was in Heat 1 and the race was pretty unremarkable, I finished in first place while trying my best to conserve energy for the final. It was also the slower Heat with just myself and the second placed athlete qualifying for the final, while the rest of the finalists came from the second heat. I watched this second heat and was a lot less confident after watching the pace set by the winner and seeing how many athletes he dragged round to good times. I now had some 4 hours to wait before I was to come up against these athletes so tried take my mind off the race by watching all my friends compete in their various events. Andy Bromley won the 80yd hurdles while Chris Houston won the 220yds.

Eventually the time came for the mile event. To be honest the race itself went by in a blur. I just remember trying desperately to hang on to the blistering pace set by the eventual winner, and finding that on the last lap he went away from me as I went away from the rest of the field. I finished in second place in a time of 5.00.08, the quickest I had ever done, while the winner clocked 4.53.80, just 0.8 seconds outside the qualifying time for the English Championships. Pleased with my time but disappointed that I did not win, I returned to school with one more chance to qualify for the English Championships at a Northern Counties meeting where I would represent Cheshire. The county meeting was a further step up in terms of competition and apart from a brief few yards in front at the start of the third lap I was swallowed up and finished fifth from ten athletes, missing the required 4.53 qualifying time by four seconds. I had given it my all, finished with a personal best, but realised that at that time I was just not good enough for the All England Championships.

Once again my confidence took a big hit and I was bitterly disappointed as I felt I was just not good enough, even though I was just 4 seconds away from qualification. Back at school I still received lots of congratulations but felt I had let the school down. The only consolation was that even if I had qualified, I would have been unable to compete in the English Championships. This was due to an event that was to change my life completely and put me in a situation that was way out of my comfort zone. This event would turn me into a very surly, moody and unhappy individual for quite some time.

Mum and Dad must have wondered what had happened to turn me into such a miserable teenager, but there was the answer, I was a teenager, and don't all teenagers turn into surly, moody, self centred people at some time during those teen years. This change of circumstances would also stall my progress as an athlete for quite some time.

4   1-BROCKHOLE TO MARDALE

"Jogging is for people who aren't intelligent enough to watch television."
-Victoria Wood

Finally the horn sounded for the start of the race. We ran down to the shores of Lake Windermere then along the shoreline for a few yards before turning away and back through the field to run under the Start/Finish banner again. Lots of shouts and cheers echoed through the clear air of the Lakeland morning as we headed out to cross the main A591 and start our first climb of the day on a very rough, bumpy and stony track towards Troutbeck.

Bodies suddenly packed together as over a hundred runners tried to squeeze into the narrow confines of the track. Any head torch was rendered useless for the first mile or so as the mass of bodies stumbled and bumbled their way up the hill. Those of us not in the front few quickly slowed to a walk and then a shuffle before we finally had enough space to break into a jog. Even then the loose rocky track meant there was a lot of cursing as runners stumbled along. It was a fair distance before we got running and by this time there seemed to be a lot of bodies in front of me and not too many behind. Once I got running I started to settle and felt happy that I had left my head torch in my bag as there was now enough light to see the terrain before me.

The first checkpoint was six miles away at Kentmere and involved four hundred and fifty metres of climb over the first pass of the day, Garburn. I was not feeling at my best during this section and struggled to get any sort of rhythm going, my legs felt heavy and I lacked any sort of conviction about what lay ahead of me. Feeling a bit out of sorts at the start of a race seemed to be something normal for me as I got older. I found that it took me about twenty to thirty minutes to get my legs going and settle into a race.

    The thing that kept me going in this event was the thought of plenty of refreshments at Kentmere, food and drink were always good motivators. I finally arrived at the Kentmere Institute after one hour and twenty seven minutes of pretty average running. The light was now good and above was a clear blue sky which promised a dry and sunny day ahead. This sort of weather did not occur too often in The Lake District, but when it did it meant the views were going to be awesome. Even though we were not going over the mountain tops the high elevation of this event meant we were going to be treated to the best of this mountain scenery.

    My stop at the checkpoint was very brief as I took on fluids before venturing out into the bright Lakeland sunshine. Still not feeling at my best I soldiered on knowing that ahead of me lay the highest pass of the day, Nan Bield, which at a height of six hundred and forty metres, would deliver us to the next checkpoint at Mardale Head. After leaving Kentmere we crossed to the right hand side of the valley and commenced the long slog up over the pass. I could see quite a long way ahead and there were lots of runners still in front of me. After a while and below to my left I could see Kentmere Reservoir. The Kentmere Horseshoe is one of the few Lake District walks I had not done but looking up the valley on this fine morning I promised myself I would complete this walk on one of my Lakeland visits. I adopted my usual approach to the climb, which was to just keep my head down and run where I could but also walk sections that were too steep. About two thirds of the way up I was beginning to feel I was getting into a rhythm when I stumbled and went crashing to the ground cracking my knee against a rock. The pain shot through my knee and my instant reaction was to get to my feet and try and continue but the pain was quite intense so I sat for a minute and hoped the pain would fade. Passing runners stopped to ask if I was ok and did I need anything. I told them I was fine I just needed the pain to die down. As I sat there I wondered if my race was to be over before it had really started. I looked at my knee and it was bleeding and looked a bit red and swollen. I wiped away the blood, got to my feet and started walking. It was still very painful but I assured myself that there was no real damage and after a couple of minutes managed to get running again. Although my knee was still paining me I felt I was beginning to get into the zone and was actually starting to to feel much more positive. I began to catch and overtake a few runners, which is always a boost, although I was very conscious that the race was still in its infancy and there was still a lot of running to be done.

We reached the top of the pass and I felt confident I could gain a few more places on the descent to the checkpoint at Mardale Head. My downhill ability on his type of terrain had improved a lot over the years due to many hours of racing and training in various hill and mountain events. The top of the pass also presented us with the first stunning view of the day. Small Water and Hawsewater Reservoir from the top were magnificent, the sun was reflecting off the water and the air was so clear. On each side of us sat the imposing summits Harter Fell and Mardale Ill Bell. My spirits were lifted by the beauty of the scene before me and with all thoughts of my painful knee all but gone, I set off on the descent. The track down to Mardale is quite rocky and technical but I was moving well and feeling confident. I started to pick up the pace and arrived at the bottom in good time.

As I arrived at the checkpoint a marshal ran over and asked if I was ok, I said I was fine and he then asked about my knee. I had forgotten about this even though it was still hurting a bit and as I looked down I could understand his concern, as my leg was covered in blood. I wiped away the blood and there was a small cut across the kneecap and it was a little bit swollen but otherwise it was fine. I looked around me at this familiar location. I had walked this area quite a few times over the years and had even started a mountain marathon from this car park in 2001, and although most of my walks and runs had been on the mountains surrounding the reservoir I was looking forward to my first time along the track on the western shore of the lake.

Runners were arriving in quick succession at this checkpoint so I quickly took on fluids along with a banana before heading off along the head of Haweswater Reservoir towards the next checkpoint at the village of Bampton, hoping my knee, stamina and confidence would hold out.

Distance covered 11.3 miles
Time taken 2hrs 57mins 35secs
Overall position at Kentmere 75th
Overall position at Mardale Head 61st

5   A WORLD AWAY

"I could feel my anger dissipating as the miles went by--you can't run and stay mad!"
— Kathrine Switzer

It was half way through my third year at Overleigh when Mum and Dad called us together and announced that we were emigrating to South Africa. Uncle George and Auntie Marg had done so a few months earlier and we were to follow, Dad would be working with his brother once again. This came as a complete shock to us kids. Both Allen and I protested and said we did not want to go, Allen was especially obstinate as he felt so settled in Chester, but there was no turning back. We would leave for South Africa in July 1968. I knew nothing about the country and was even oblivious to the apartheid regime or what it meant.

I was a fourteen year old who had discovered girls and, like most teenagers, I thought the whole world revolved around me. Poor Mum and Dad had to cope with two moody teenagers who were both becoming very troublesome. I resented my parents for wanting to take me away from Chester and could not understand why they wanted to do it. I had a girlfriend and had started to spend too much time with her. As the move date was approaching I started to lose interest in my school work and at the end of the year I finished in the bottom few in my class. I normally finished in the top five or six and my parents were at a loss as to why I was struggling academically

As well as my school work my relationship with my parents had also deteriorated. I was staying out later and was constantly coming home up to an hour after I should have. This led to me eventually being grounded for a couple of weeks. This seemed to make me even worse and in our last week, when we were due to go and stay with family in Liverpool before the journey to South Africa, I told them I wanted to spend a last night at Micky Worrall's. They let me and told me they would pick me up the following evening, but I had lied to them and stayed over at my girlfriend's. I told my girlfriend's parents that Mum and Dad knew but the reality was that Mum and Dad had forbidden me from seeing her quite a few weeks before but I had been seeing her behind their backs. When Dad came to pick me up at Micky's house I was not there and he guessed where I was. I could see he was hurt and disappointed that I had lied to him but he said nothing as we made our way back to Liverpool. I guess it was pointless arguing about it, we were about to start the six thousand mile, two week trip to Johannesburg the following day.

Looking back on that time I now realise that if we had stayed in Chester I would probably have ended up married with a couple of kids by the time I was twenty. Although the sporting side of things was still good I was becoming distracted, my school work was suffering and I needed a kick up the backside to wake me up. The move to South Africa was very difficult initially, I was still the moody teenager and Allen was even worse, he eventually returned to the UK nine months later after several battles with Mum and Dad.

As a fourteen year old I will admit I did not see what was going on around me. As all teenagers I was totally self centred and it was only when I returned some years later that I fully understood the injustice of the South African regime. I can remember the first time I stood on a bus stop that had a sign saying 'Whites Only' and not really thinking what this meant. I was more worried about my first day at school and the sort of reception I was going to get on the school bus. I had been told that the girls especially liked to embarrass new starts as much as they could. With me still being this very shy and self conscious individual I was dreading that first journey, and true to form, once on the bus they really went to town on me. I sat there cringing and embarrassed by their antics and comments and hated every minute of that journey. This form of mental bullying went on for the first week or so and as I did not react, they got bored and finally left me alone. I know it sounds awful but I did become good friends with most of those girls and their teasing was just to test my character.

Nevertheless looking back at life in South Africa in the late 60's and early 70's it was very different to the UK. White people held all the positions of power and had superior housing, buses, trains, schools and even sporting events and venues. This was a strange set up but I just accepted that this was the way life was. Even when I started my apprenticeship Native Africans were only allowed to work in the factory as cleaners or had menial jobs in the canteens. The really strange thing was being referred to as 'boss', even though I was only a teenager. During this time in Africa I took part in lots of sporting events but never against a Native African.

Over the initial 18 months of my time there I tried to keep abreast of events in Chester by writing to my friend since junior school, John Relish. John was the only person in Chester with whom I would correspond on a regular basis. It was good to keep in touch but unfortunately most of what he was telling me was making me worse. He would tell me which players from our team were having trials at football clubs and this just made me feel awful about being in South Africa while they were all getting the opportunities I longed for. I was playing for the school football team and even competed in a couple of mile events for the school but my heart was not really in it. Mostly I was just feeling sorry for myself instead of getting on with life. Having said this, my school work started to improve again and a few of the teachers tried to encourage me to stay on for the extra two years and then go on to university. I was having none of this and left school at the earliest opportunity, which was December 1969. Dad had arranged for me to start as an apprentice sheet metal worker in January 1970 and I was not going to pass up this chance. Looking back this was a bit short sighted but at the time I hated the school life and could not wait to get out of it.

. The next few years consisted of drink, girls and a brief spell of drug experimentation which was soon abandoned and never really got beyond the smoking element. I was still a very keen footballer and maintained a high level of fitness and this fitness never really left me, because I always worked hard in training. Even during spells when my drinking became excessive and I was smoking weed nearly every day I was still managing to perform well. When you are young it seems your body can take this punishment and recover very quickly. Football had become my main focus and I worked hard at this and reached a reasonable standard. The team I played for was the works team called Atlas Aircraft. The first team reached what was the equivalent of the Conference League standard here in England. It was at this time that I had my short spell with the first team and was drinking to calm my nerves. There were some very good players in this team and again I always felt I was not good enough, hence the drinking to help me cope. The sad thing is I had shown in training that I was good enough, but as I was a player who did not respond well to a rollicking and I needed that arm around the shoulder I never progressed beyond the reserve team.

After finishing my apprenticeship I gained three years valuable experience as a tradesman while earning very good money. I had a hankering for a return to the UK, but where would I go? My old school mates had all moved on with their lives, John Relish was playing professionally with Newport County, so I felt a return to Chester would be pointless. Even my brother Allen had returned to South Africa a couple of years earlier as a married man.

Then in 1974 I met two lads from Bristol who were working in South Africa on a twelve month contract, and were working at the same factory as Allen. I had been away on a two month tour of Europe in a Volkswagen campervan with my best mate Bernie and two Aussies, Springy and Algy. This trip made my restlessness even worse. I had had a great time which included three weeks in the UK and my first ever trip to the Lake District.

I remember thinking what a beautiful place this was as I viewed it from the comfort of a ferry or a tour bus. Little did I know how attached I would become to this fantastic area of Britain in later years, especially in regards to my running. When I returned to South Africa my brother introduced me to Ian and Ian. To avoid confusion we named them big Ian and little Ian. Little Ian played in the same football team as me and as I was a single man they wanted me to introduce them to the local nightlife. Unfortunately the nightlife in South Africa was nothing like they were used to in the UK. On one occasion we went into a night club in Hillbrow, Johannesburg, which was supposed to be the best place for clubs and pubs, and apart from a girl working behind the bar there were only two girls in the whole place. With about fifty blokes in there you can imagine how much attention the girls got. This scenario was not unusual. Girls just did not go out unless they were with their boyfriend or on a date. Consequently most places were packed with men who just got wrecked. There were plenty of bars in the Johannesburg area but no women. The two Ian's were not impressed and it was obvious from early on that they were going to hightail it back to England at the earliest opportunity.

When they returned to the UK they asked me over to stay in Bristol for a few weeks. I took up the offer and we had two weeks in Spain with all their friends as well as a couple of weeks in Bristol. I had a great time and upon my return to South Africa I told my parents I was going back to the UK and I was going to Bristol to live. They weren't too surprised and I spent the next twelve months working as many hours as I could while saving for my new venture. The time came for me to leave and although I was very nervous I was sure I was doing the right thing. My mum and dad were very supportive and wished me well and told me to keep in touch, which in itself was quite difficult in those days with no mobile phones or any of the social media apps that are around today. It was old fashioned letter writing, and that is not easy. I found that I never really wrote often enough and found it quite a chore, but on the other side of the coin, I loved receiving letters from them.

I returned to the UK in March 1976, just in time for the best summer in living memory. I found work within a few weeks and settled in to my new environment very quickly. Just a few months later my brother Allen got in touch to say he was getting a divorce and would be returning to the UK. He also decided he wanted to live in Bristol and, along with my friend Martin, I set about trying to find a decent sized flat for the three of us.

I was working for a company called Parnalls and also started playing for their football team. When I joined we were in the fourth division of the Bristol and District League. We managed to get a good team together and over the next few seasons won successive promotions and ended up in the first division. These were probably my best football years. I was comfortable with the team and the players so my confidence grew. I won player of the year on two occasions and was also getting a few goals each season, the player of the year award was particularly satisfying because it was the players who voted for the winner of this award. The fact that my team mates, rather than the club committee, voted for me meant an awful lot to me. Once again this is me searching for acceptance and popularity.

As I approached thirty I started to get a few problems with my knees and following a visit to the doctor he recommended I try running in between matches. I started this and found I began to really enjoy it. This situation was to reignite my love of running and shape me as an athlete and a person. I was to encounter a few setbacks but running became a huge part of my life and some may say I became obsessed with it, but I loved it and the whole ethos of the sport. It was just so refreshing to run past someone and hear them say 'well done, keep going' instead of them trying to kick lumps out of me, as was the case in football matches. The year was 1981 and the running boom was well and truly on. Suddenly marathon races were popping up all over the place and I decided I wanted to try one.

6 MARATHON TALK

"Remember, the second most important thing to choosing the right shoe, is choosing the left one."
- High school coach to his runners

At this time I was working at Rolls Royce in Bristol and decided I wanted to have a crack at a marathon. I convinced a work colleague, Les Willet, that a marathon would be a great thing to have a go at. Les was mainly a footballer like myself, but eventually he agreed, so together we had a look at the running calendar and set our sights on the Winchester Marathon.

We were both still playing football but managed to fit in a few runs around matches. I can't really remember too much about my preparation but it was obviously wholly inadequate. I think the longest distance I ran was about 13 miles but with the football matches I felt this would be enough. My abiding memory of the race was running with Les at thirteen miles and both of us commenting on how good we felt. Within two miles of this statement we were introduced to the world of marathon running as the wheels came off and someone stole my legs and gave me an old knackered pair instead. I did not understand at the time but this condition is called 'hitting the wall'. This was my first experience of this strange phenomena but it was certainly not going to be my last. It is difficult to explain to someone how you can be running at, say eight minute miles, then out of the blue you struggle to run twelve minute miles. This was what happened to us as Les started to drop back and I was really struggling. I don't know why but I had this thing in my head that said unless I ran the whole way then I had not done a marathon. Even when I wanted a pee, around the sixteen mile mark, I waited for a quiet spot found a way to aim over to the side whilst still running, and managed to accomplish the whole thing without peeing all down my leg. I battled on through another torturous ten miles and although I was hardly moving above walking pace, I crossed the line in 3hrs 45mins, Les finished about fifteen minutes behind me.

I did not realise how tired a body can feel until I finished that marathon. We were both elated at completing but our bodies were wrecked and the drive back to Bristol in my Mini was very painful. We stopped at one point to get a drink and both struggled so get out and back into the car. For days my legs ached while the rest of me just felt so tired. I had always seen myself as very fit, as I had played football twice a week for years. I even remember one year, because of bad weather, quite a few games were cancelled so we ended up having to play three or four evenings a week to catch up, as well as playing back to back games on a Sunday morning. Even this did not prepare me for the utter exhaustion I felt after the marathon.

My brother rang me in the evening after the race to ask how it went and I told him how painful the whole experience was. He was keen to have a go at one himself and asked me if I would ever do another one. Despite the pain of that first one I did not hesitate in saying yes. I was determined to have another go but this time my preparation would be much better. He did not seem to be put off by my tales of pain and hurt so we decided to try and find a race we could both run.

A quick look at the calendar and Kingswood Marathon was scheduled for 23 May 1982. Kingswood is a district in Bristol so this would be on familiar territory. The race had a reputation of being very tough. It was a two lap course which included plenty of hills including the fearsome Hanham Road on both laps, the second time at the twenty two mile mark. We both entered the race and starting our training.

I was determined to train further, faster and longer for this event. It was also the first event that I would use to collect sponsorship money from my work mates. I was running fairly regularly at this time but stepped into my marathon training in April. It was around this time that I discovered that I was asthmatic. I had suffered with hay fever since I was a teenager but up until now it had never affected my breathing, but I now discovered that if I did too much speed work through the summer months then I could be prone to asthma attacks. This is probably the reason the majority of my personal best's were achieved in Spring and Autumn. Most of the time I was fine but on the odd occasion, either during a race or a particularly tough training session, I would have to stop and walk until I recovered.

The other thing I started doing at this time was to keep a running diary. This diary became something I used throughout my running and, sad individual that I am, I have kept all of these hand written volumes dating back to 1982. I moved across to using computer software for my diaries in 1995 but lost a couple of years when I had a computer crash, but have most of my diaries from 1982 to present day. My initial attempt was fairly basic. I just recorded how far, what time and minutes per mile, in a small diary I had received from a book club. Later the information became a bit more detailed, weather conditions, how my asthma was, how I felt physically and split times. I also started each year with a review of the previous year and target setting for the coming twelve months.

What those early diaries show is how naive I was. I could not do any training on Saturday or Sunday because of football, so ended up doing my long runs on Monday evenings. This was my training for the 8 weeks leading up to Kingswood. In my first three weeks I played six matches and averaged thirty miles per week. My longest run was eighteen miles. In my next three weeks I played ten matches and only ran a total of forty two miles, my longest run was twelve miles. In my final two weeks I did eighty seven miles which included two long runs of eighteen and nineteen miles. The nineteen miles was the furthest I had run in my preparation and I did this just a week before the race. When I look back now I wonder how I ever got into my head that this was the way to prepare for a marathon, but because I was still a footballer who ran, I was missing the benefit of being around people who had marathon experience and could advise me on the best way to prepare. I mean, how difficult could it be, surely I just needed to run more often. It would be a lot of miles and a lot of pain before I started to really understand what was required to get myself ready for an event.

Eventually marathon number two had arrived and I felt I was much better prepared. The event went very well even though I faded badly after twenty miles due to my training stupidity. I crossed the line in 3:22:11 and was really happy with this. My brother Allen however did even better. He finished two minutes ahead of me in 3:20. This was to be the quickest marathon he ever ran, because it was the only marathon he ever ran. He decided that once was enough and even though he ran numerous races after this, he never ran another marathon. Instead he went back to football and continued to play local league football up to the age of sixty.

So with two marathons done and an improvement of over twenty minutes, I felt I could do even better and set about trying to learn how to tackle this epic distance. Even though my preparation was pretty basic I had improved a lot and did not suffer as bad as after my first marathon. I even started to dream of a sub three hour marathon. This, for me, would be the absolute pinnacle of marathon running. If I could achieve this then I would be in the same hour as the world record holder at that time, Rob De Castella.

This was an era of marathon records and great marathon heroes, but the one who inspired me the most was Steve Jones. Here was a Welshman who had determination like I had never seen before. Steve Jones had worked his way on to the marathon scene via 10,000 metre track events. He showed a spirit that you could only admire and even when hit by stomach cramps at London 1985 he ran on to victory. He ran the 1984 Chicago Marathon and won the event, setting a new world record time of 2:08:05. A look at Jones' training schedule reveals just how determined he was to be prepared. In the five weeks prior to the event, Jones put in the hard miles running 100, 84, 71, 71 and

100 miles leading up to the race.

Buoyed by the success of Kingswood I entered the Bristol marathon which was just nine weeks after Kingswood. I took a week off running after Kingswood then slowly started to build up the miles. I did a half marathon three weeks later and just missed out on a sub 1:30 so was feeling confident about Bristol. Once again I did all the wrong things, my highest mileage week, sixty miles, was done two weeks before the race and in my final week I clocked up too many miles.

Race day was Sunday 25 July 1982, the course was a simple out and back along the Portway to Avonmouth. This road ran for miles along the River Avon out of Bristol to Avonmouth Docks. The problem with this was it was straight and boring, and while you were still running out you could see the lead runners coming back in.

The start was overcast and by five miles I was going well, hitting seven minutes per mile and feeling good. The day gradually warmed and turned into the hottest day so far that year. By fourteen miles I thought I was going to melt, by eighteen miles I was shuffling along at ten minutes per mile and at a drink station at twenty two miles I sat down and said "that's it, I'm done". I had walked off and on since twenty miles and just gave up. I was transported back to the start in a Land Rover with two or three other drop outs and the driver turned to us and said "why did you drop out, are you injured?". I did not know what to say because, when I dropped out I felt as though I could not run another yard, yet thirty minutes later in the car going back to the start I felt ok. So why did I bail? Yes, I was very tired because I had not trained correctly, but a combination of the heat, my inability to "Tough it Out" and the thought of getting back in a time that was going to be even slower than my first marathon, never mind my dream of sub three, was something I could not face up to. Lots of people at work had sponsored me and they all knew I was aiming to get close to three hours. They all kindly handed over their sponsorship money even though I had to explain to each what had gone wrong. I blamed it on the heat and the monotonous, boring course. Again I did not understand what had happened but I had hit the wall and there is no coming back from that during a race.

The failure at Bristol was a real blow and I gave up running for quite a time. I had decided I was not cut out for this marathon lark, and threw myself back into football. There was to follow another major upheaval in my life before I returned to running over twelve months later, but without this dramatic change I am not sure that I would ever have started running again. The Bristol failure had hit me and my confidence very hard and I was not sure I could face that sort of failure again.

7 TIME FOR A CHANGE

"Running should be a lifelong activity. Approach it patiently and intelligently, and it will reward you for a long, long time."
-Michael Sargent

Britain in the early eighties was a tough place to live. I had been married for a couple of years and had bought a small three bedroom end terrace house in Brislington, Bristol. Interest rates had been dropping slightly but were still in double figures and unemployment was at three million. Although I had a good job at Rolls-Royce I felt we needed a change plus the opportunity to earn good money for a few years so my thoughts turned to South Africa. Mum and Dad were still there and I felt sure we could go there for a few years to make some money. I persuaded my wife that it would be worth it and so we sold up and arranged to travel to Johannesburg in January 1983.

My return to South Africa meant I got to spend lots of time with family, I re-discovered my love of running and finally my son, Lee was born. Of all the events in my life the birth of my son was the proudest and happiest. We had been trying for a few years without success and after a few visits to a specialist in Johannesburg he informed us that we were pretty much incompatible with regards to having children. I had a low sperm count, which was a result of a bout of mumps from my childhood, and Lesley produced an excess of fluid that killed off sperm in the womb. The doctor was still confident that he could help and six months later Lesley became pregnant. We were overjoyed and could not wait for the birth. There was a bit of panic when Lesley started to lose blood three months into the pregnancy and after a visit to hospital we thought she had lost the baby. After a worrying wait the doctor informed us that she had lost a twin. They told us that Lee was fine and we should not worry. The rest of the pregnancy went fairly smoothly and Lee was born on 26th June 1984. He was a couple of weeks premature so was in intensive care for the first week of his life. When the time came to take him home we were so nervous, suddenly this tiny fragile thing was our sole responsibility and we were left to get on with it. Of course we had the support of family and friends but those first few weeks were a very anxious period. With the support of my family we coped and became more confident with our new arrival. It was great seeing family again and spending time with them.

South Africa itself was changing and was very different from the South Africa I had encountered during my first spell there. Apartheid was still law but there were many changes going on. The engineering company I worked for was now taking on Native Africans as apprentices and I worked alongside one of these newly trained artisans. His name was Joseph and he was married with two children. We struck up a good friendship and spoke to each other a lot about work, about family and about life in general. I told him how much change I felt had happened since I last lived here. He agreed that a lot of positive things that happened but then pointed out that at the end of the day he would be going home on the 'Blacks Only' bus to the township whereas I would be driving home to my nice home on a 'Whites Only' estate. This was the first time I had really spoken to someone who, in the eyes of the South African government, was classed as black, so did not have the same rights as myself. He could now work alongside me doing the same job, but earned less money and could not buy a house where I lived or travel on the same bus or train as myself. This situation had to end and I was just hoping that it could end without violence or bloodshed.

Shortly after arriving in South Africa I met a guy called Mick King. I had played alongside Mick in the Atlas football team in the early seventies. Mick was a larger than life cockney character who loved his football but hated training. As I have already stated I used to work really hard in training, but Mick avoided the hard work as much as he could. He would even hide behind things while all the running and sprinting went on, then would rejoin the group when we started playing a game.

You can imagine how surprised I was when he told me he had given up football and started running. He was with a local club and said he was really enjoying it. I mentioned my running exploits to date and he invited me along to his club for a run. I decided to take up his offer and I guess this was the turning point in my running life. I went along to the club and got talking with lots of other people who loved their running. While running in the UK I had done the majority of my training on my own and never even thought about joining a club. I began to realise that being a member of a club was vital if you wanted to improve. The club has the structure, the training and the experienced runners which make up the perfect environment for running success.

My cousin Mike was also living close by and was running as well. We both joined Atlas running club and started some regular training. This regular, structured training brought immediate benefits as my times started to come down which was all down to the club and its members. Talking with these people was like a breath of fresh air, they all had tales of running exploits, successes and failures, and you could not help but get caught up in the atmosphere and excitement of racing.

There were lots of really good runners at the club and I was keen to learn as much as I could from them. I steadily built up my mileage and did as many club long runs as I could. I still played a bit of football but gave that up after I received a punch in the face during one match. I finished up in hospital and nearly lost the sight in my right eye. Two weeks of complete rest and five stitches in my eyebrow later, I was able to return to work. Although I played a couple of times after this incident my heart was not in it and I decided to call it a day and concentrate on running.

Where the UK had the London Marathon as its premier event, South Africa had the Comrades Marathon. This event was started in 1921 by Victor Clapham to commemorate his fallen Comrades from the Great War. It has taken place every year since then except for the period of the Second World War. In June 1984 the race attracted five thousand runners. Not as big as London you may say but the remarkable thing about the Comrades is that it is raced over a distance that is more than a double marathon. The distance is not always the same each year because of road works and diversions, but it is always run between the cities of Durban and Pietermaritzburg over an approximate distance of 90Km (55 miles). It is also different in that it is run from Pietermaritzburg to Durban one year, the 'down run', and Durban to Pietermaritzburg, the following year, the 'up run'. The runs were classed 'up' and 'down' because Durban is on the coast so is at sea level, whereas Pietermaritzburg is some two thousand feet above sea level. The race is now the biggest Ultra Marathon in the world and entries are capped at twenty thousand. In the 1980's the cut off time was eleven hours but has now been extended to twelve hours. It would be easy to assume that the 'up run' was the tougher event but the many people I had spoken to said that although the down run was usually quicker they always suffered more after the 'down run' and it always took longer to recover.

If Steve Jones was my marathon hero then Bruce Fordyce was my Ultra marathon hero. Bruce was the most famous Comrades runner of that modern era. Bruce was Comrades king from 1981 to 1988 when he won it in successive years. In 1987 he broke the down record with a time of 5:24:07. Then in 1988 he broke the record for the up run with a time of 5:27:42. In 1989 the winner was Sam Tshabalala, but in 1990 Bruce returned to reclaim his crown. Schoolteacher Frith van der Merwe won the woman's race in 1988 in a time of 6:32:56. In 1989, Van der Merwe ran 5:54:43, obliterating the women's record and finishing fifteenth overall.

Wally Hayward was another Comrades legend winning it for the first time in 1930 aged 21. He then went on to compete in shorter events before returning in 1940 as a 41 year old. He shocked everybody by taking the lead at halfway and going on to break the record in a time of six hours forty six minutes. In 1988 Wally Hayward entered the race at the age of 79 and finished in an amazing 9:44:15. He repeated the feat in the 1989 Comrades, where he completed the race with only two minutes to spare and at the age of 80 became the oldest man to complete the Comrades. Wally Hayward died in May 2006 at the age of 97.

This was the event that all the club runners spoke about and trained for each year, so at the start of 1984 I took the plunge and entered the Comrades Marathon. This year would be a 'down' year and I had decided to throw myself into my training and take part in this awesome event. This would mean lots of miles and lots of hours out running. Lesley was pregnant with Lee and was due in early July and as the race was on the first of June it would be out of the way before the birth.

Looking back at the small diary I kept at the time the highest weekly mileage I did in preparation was seventy five miles, which I did in the middle of April. For a 56 mile race this was probably far too little but I was feeling and running really well. I had run a half marathon personal best, and also completed my first ultra the 'Milo Korki' 56k. This event was a real eye opener for me. I started very well but once I got beyond the marathon distance it became a very painful experience. I put this down to the fact that I was in the middle of my training for comrades and so was running on tired legs. I finished in what I felt was a reasonable time, but I now realised how tough Comrades was going to be. There was another 40k on top of the Milo distance and the Milo was the toughest event I had done up to that time. I competed in quite a few other races over all sorts of distances and recorded some good times, so all in all I felt the training was going well. The lack of my miles was not apparent to me at the time and this was something I would learn about as I ran more and more. Within that training I had also done a marathon at Sun City in just over three hours. At the time this was my best marathon time and I should have been ecstatic about this but the story of the race meant I came away feeling exhausted, deflated and a little annoyed.

8   MARATHON COMRADES

"Now if you are going to win any battle you have to do one thing. You have to make the mind run the body. Never let the body tell the mind what to do. The body will always give up. It is always tired in the morning, noon and night. But the body is never tired if the mind is not tired."
— George S Patton

It was Saturday 17th March at Sun City and I felt that this might be the sub three marathon I had dreamt of. During the past few months at club runs I had got talking to another athlete, Dudley, about my sub three dream. Dudley was a regular sub three marathoner and suggested I should run with him at the forthcoming Sun City marathon. This fitted in well with my comrades training so along, with another three or four club athletes, including John McGowan we put ourselves in his hands.

John and I had spent a lot of time training together and were very closely matched. He was from the north of England and still had a really strong accent. We hit it off and spoke a lot about our marathon hopes. We did quite a few races together and ran about the same pace. We also felt that Sun City would be really good for both of us, and would also be good preparation for our attempt at Comrades success.

Dudley insisted that he would be the only one wearing a watch and as there were no time clocks on the course, we would not be able to tell if we were ahead or behind schedule. The course was a straightforward out and back and started at six in the morning to avoid the worst of the heat. We gathered at the start feeling anxious but confident that Dudley would pull us through in less than three hours. The first half of the race went very smoothly, we even picked up a few more runners who joined our three hour 'bus'. At this point I think I need to explain the term 'bus' in a running context. It was term used in South

Africa when a group of like minded runners decided to run together to achieve a particular target, hence the term 'bus'. Two thirds into the race and people started drop off the back of the 'bus'. I was also beginning to feel the heat and was struggling to hang on. Dudley tried to keep the pace going but by twenty two miles there was just John, Dudley and myself left. What happened next shocked me a bit. With John and me now really struggling, Dudley looked at his watch and decided to leave us, he ran off leaving us trailing in his wake. I tried to stay with him but failed and I finally crawled across the line totally spent having missed the three hour mark by just a couple of minutes. The after effects were a touch of sunstroke and I had to lie down for nearly an hour feeling light headed and nauseous. John came in not far behind me looking and feeling as bad as myself. There was no sign of Dudley so we both found a place in the shade and sat down to recover.

We both should have been feeling elated at the times we had achieved, but I just felt awful and was really disappointed at having missed the three hour mark. How could this have happened when before the race I had felt I was so well prepared.

Sometime later I found Dudley and asked him why he had left me and John. "I have not taken over three hours for a marathon in years, and I was not going to today". I felt this was a bit selfish of him but asked why he felt it had all gone so wrong in the second half. "I don't really know" he replied "because at half way we were six minutes ahead of schedule". I could not believe what I was hearing, my half marathon best was one hour twenty four and this idiot had taken us through in that time for a marathon. This was the first inkling I had about this type of runner and just because someone could run fast, it did not necessarily make them an intelligent runner.

Myself and John came away from Sun City bitterly disappointed but we threw ourselves back into Comrades training and put the incident to the back our minds. Marathons would have to take a back seat until we had completed Comrades.

The build up to Comrades was an exciting time, myself and

John McGowan had done a lot miles together and we were both quietly confident about the race. The target we were going to aim for was seven and a half hours. This would earn us the much coveted silver medal. Over seven and a half hours would get us a bronze medal. The silver medal would mean we would have to run two marathons in under three hours forty five minutes, a tough challenge but we were up for it.

The event took place on a bank holiday weekend so all the club's competitors went down to Durban for the weekend. Cars would then ferry us up to Pietermaritzburg for the start. This was a journey of around an hour and as the race started at 6.30 we were up and on our way by 4am. The temperature in Pietermaritzburg at the start was -1 and most athletes had extra layers of clothing that they would discard en route because the temperature would rise to twenty four degrees by the time we reached Durban. To be honest the first half of the race passed me by a little. Myself and John maintained our three hour forty five minute marathon pace and as we entered the second half of the race we were still feeling good. Over the next ten miles was where it all went wrong. My leg muscles started to tighten as the constant running downhill wrecked my quads. Don't get me wrong there are plenty of climbs on the 'down run' but the constant downhill running was my undoing. By forty miles I was unable to run downhill, my quads were screaming at me. John tried to keep me going and offered words of encouragement, as did other athletes. One individual suggested I walk backwards down the most severe hills. I really did not think this was a good idea, unlike another runner who overheard us. He turned round and stared walking backwards and within five yards was firmly planted on his backside, "rubbish idea that" he muttered as he got gingerly to his feet. I certainly wasn't the only one walking down the hills lots of other athletes were going through the same pain as me. Our dream of a silver medal was fast disappearing and I was beginning to have serious doubts about even finishing the race.

John was certainly stronger than me during this part of the

race but refused to go ahead saying we had trained together so we would finish together. We kept going and slowly I started feel better as I found my legs again. With about seven miles to go it was now John's turn to struggle, I was feeling much better and I returned the favour by giving him as much encouragement as possible. With just a few miles to go we stuck together and when we entered the stadium with just one lap of the track to go, we could not believe how many people were in the stadium. There were thousands of people and the noise they made was incredible, we felt as though we were winning the race. We crossed the line triumphantly in a time of 8.28.18 and I had not felt this exhausted since my first marathon but I was so proud to have completed this historic race. The winner that year was, of course, Bruce Fordyce.

After the race we found our club mates and sat down to watch the rest of the event. This is why the stadium was so full, all the finishers sat in the stands to watch the rest of the race unfold. As the cut off time approaches, which was eleven hours in 1984, you can feel the tension rising. This is because at Comrades if you do not make the cut off time you get nothing, no medal and no name in the results list. As this time approaches and athletes are stumbling into the stadium the crowd just roars them on. They still have four hundred meters to go once in the stadium and in the condition they are in this equates to a couple of minutes. Some are still running, some are walking, some are crawling and some even stop to take it all in, but the crowd do not let them stop for long as they will them towards the finish line. A minute before the cut off time an official walks on to the track and stands with their back to the runners on the finish line. With ten seconds to go the crowd starts the countdown, the official raises his arm and in his hand is a starting pistol. At the end of the countdown he fires the gun while other officials run across the track with barrier tape to prevent anyone else crossing the finish line. In 1984 seven thousand one hundred and five runners made the cut off but I have no idea how many just missed out. The only consolation for the person who is left just metres from the line when the gun goes is the media attention. Everyone wants to know where they are from and will they be back next year. If I recall correctly Adidas interviewed this person and promised to sponsor them if they came back the following year, so not a bad result after all.

As I had been told before the race, it took my legs a long time to recover from this ordeal, but I had come through and this showed I had mental strength. There were many times during the race that I felt like quitting but a combination of my mental strength and John McGowan pulled me through. Thank you John I don't think I could have completed this race without you along side me.

So what did I do after Comrades? Well for two weeks I did nothing at all then I did a couple of steady runs before taking part in a road relay where I chalked up an 8km best time of 28.50.

Three weeks after the event Lee was born. Even with the birth of Lee I still managed to keep the running momentum I had gained from my Comrades preparation. I would get up at four in the morning a couple of times a week and go out for a ten to fifteen mile run. I would then go home, shower and make my way to work. I managed to take part in most of our club runs, mainly because our long runs were held very early on a Saturday morning and we also did time trials (4k & 8k) once a week in the evening, just half a mile away from where I lived.

One by product of Comrades was quite a bit of knee pain. I tried to ignore it but eventually I had to go to the doctor who diagnosed tendonitis. This meant complete rest. It was nearly four weeks before I started running steadily again, but I soon managed to increase the mileage as I tried to set myself up for another attempt at a sub three marathon.

My target for a sub three attempt was the Johnson Crane Marathon in late January 1985. In preparation for this I increased my long runs and competed in a few races which included at personal best over 15km (59.31). I then decided on another marathon just two weeks before the Johnson Crane. I had got talking to a few more runners at the club and they suggested I go with them to a marathon race where they were planning to run at 3.10 pace. Again I was told not to wear a watch as they would control the pace. I was a bit unsure because of my last experience of this but they assured me that they would keep it all under control. I placed myself in their hands and took part. The race itself was very uneventful as they chatted with me as we went. I felt relaxed and comfortable but instead of dying in the second half I was still feeling relaxed. Just after twenty miles, with me still not knowing what pace I was doing they asked how I felt. I was good and felt there was more to give. They told me to hold back until twenty two miles and if I felt ok then I was to push on. I took their advice and kicked on just after twenty two miles. I did not go all out because I had another marathon to do in two weeks, but I increased my pace and crossed the line feeling I could carry on and do a few more miles. I was amazed to see I had run a 3.05 marathon so easily when at Sun City I had run 3.02 and felt I was going to die. This race gave me the confidence and the knowledge to now attack that sub three barrier. Could I finally crack it or would too many races, nerves and the occasion get to me.

9 2-MARDALE HEAD TO HOWTOWN

I've always felt that long, slow distance produces long, slow runners.
-Sebastian Coe

Looking at the OS map prior to the race the section along the western shore of Haweswater Reservoir looked as though it would be a good track followed by a couple of miles on road before reaching the Bampton village checkpoint. How wrong I was. The path on this side of the lake is a mixture of ups, downs, rocks and mud. It seemed to go on forever and a lot of runners were now beginning to struggle on this section, myself included. There was very little running done and the pain in my knee seemed to get worse. I was also getting a tingling sensation in my right foot, which I knew was my Morton's Neuroma problem. This tingling would eventually lead to numbness and then a dull ache in the bottom of my foot. The gaps between the runners were getting bigger and bigger by this time and I found myself on my own by the time I reached the road at the end of the lake. It seemed to have taken me an age to get to the far end of the lake and I had made very little headway with regards to overall position. I was beginning to think that maybe this event was just a step too far at this point. I soldiered on trying to keep positive, but the only real positive at this point was the weather. It was one of those crisp clear sunny Lakeland days where you could see for miles. The views today were going to be quite spectacular, but at this point I was struggling to get any enjoyment from it mainly because we were low down with little else but the lake to look at. My body was feeling very tired, my knee was hurting, my foot was hurting, my legs were aching and I desperately needed something to pick me up. When I reached Bampton village hall I found it had just the thing.

Sometimes in events when you feel down and out of it, it

takes just one small thing to make all the difference. At Bampton they had not one but two things that gave me a real lift. The first is quite trivial but seeing it made me feel part of this event, it also made me determined to give it my best shot. This small thing was a blackboard with the names of all the athletes in the event and a little note wishing them all the best. There was something about seeing your name alongside all the other athletes that made me feel a part of it and for me it was a real boost. I don't know if this had the same effect on any other athletes, but I would like to thank the organisers here and now for this small gesture, it was certainly the pick me up I needed.

The second thing was the nutrition. They had porridge and as I wolfed down two sachets it seemed to have a magical effect. They also had something that I had used a lot during my spell running in South Africa, flat coke. It had worked then so I decided that today I would take on as much of this, and the porridge, as I could handle, in the hope that it would give me the boost I needed. I probably spent fifteen minutes at Bampton but it was worth it. I came away feeling very positive and refreshed, the sun was shining, I was running in my favourite part of the world and I had lots of stunning scenery and countryside to look forward to in the hours ahead. What was there not to like?

As I made my way north along the road from Bampton towards Helton, I spotted another runner ahead of me. I caught him after a couple of miles, just before the turning off the road where we headed back on to the fells towards Askham Fell. We ran together for a while and chatted before I moved on ahead of him. I was now in a much more positive frame of mind, the knee pain had subsided quite substantially, my foot was just a dull throb and I felt I was enjoying the experience. The climb over Askham was not too severe, the trail was good, soft and smooth, the weather stunning and I was moving well and beginning to catch people.

This was another area I was familiar with as I had taken part in a mountain marathon here a few years earlier, and two or three of the checkpoints had been on these fells. Whilst running across Askham Fell I could see across Ullswater to the high ridge of Helvellyn. The air was so clear I felt I could reach out and touch the summit. After a couple of kilometres of nice gentle running I was making my way down under Barton Fell above Ullswater and towards the next checkpoint at Howtown. We had now been going a good few hours and on such a glorious day in the Lake District this meant lots of walkers were out and about. Occasionally I would see people ahead of me only to realise they were actually out walking. I used these people to keep me going. As I spotted them I made the effort to catch them and this momentum helped as I managed to overtake lots of walkers and a few runners before I reached Howtown. Once again the views as I started to descend to the next checkpoint were fantastic, Ullswater was shimmering in the sunshine and lots of holiday makers were out on the water. Canoes, Kayaks and ferry boats dotted all over the lake and views like this helped to distract from the aching in my legs.

The checkpoint at Howtown was quite small and manned by just a couple of people. I stopped for a brief chat and again took on board a banana and some flat coke. I was just one checkpoint away from the halfway point and I was feeling good. I looked at my watch and it was now just before noon. The 50k race would be starting about now so this meant my wife Claire would probably be an hour and a half ahead of me by the time I got to Patterdale. I was feeling good and still felt I had a chance of catching her. This positivity was completely different from my thoughts at the start as my mind had now turned from bailing at half way to running on and trying to catch Claire. What I did not realise was how tough the very demanding climb over Boredale Hause was going to be before I was to reach Patterdale. Nevertheless I definitely felt more in tune with the race and upbeat about this challenge as I left the checkpoint and made my way along the valley floor towards the Hause.

Distance covered 25.2 miles

BILL GRAHAM

Time taken 5hrs 57mins 33secs
Overall position at Bampton 60th
Overall position at Howtown 54th

10 ONE FOR THE ROAD

"The only reason I would take up jogging is so that I could hear heavy breathing again."
- Erma Bombeck

The Johnson Crane marathon took place on Sunday 27 January 1985. This was it, I was going out to try and obtain that sub three marathon I had so longed for. I had decided I was going to do it on my own. I would wear a watch and I would decide what pace I was going to run. It was time for me to stand on my own two feet and control how I ran the race. Once again this was an early start to avoid the worst of the heat that a South African summer could provide. We set off and I was soon into my stride and running at a pace that would get me through halfway in just under ninety minutes. I went through half way in one hour twenty nine minutes and thirty five seconds. This was perfect but I knew the tough miles were still ahead of me and I could not afford to get carried away. It was not a huge field but with sixteen hundred athletes it meant groups formed, running at various paces. This suited me and I latched on to a group that were going out for a sub three. Even so I checked my watch regularly to make sure the pace was not too fast.

The race progressed and I felt comfortable enough to even chat with other runners. This helped take my mind off the fact that I was trying to run quicker than I had ever done before.

The group I was with maintained this pace for the next few miles with only a couple of runners dropping off the back. This continued through to about nineteen miles with a few more dropping off the pace. I was still there and feeling good but was still waiting for that wall to come crashing into me at any moment. The nervous excitement was building and this was good because instead of dwelling on the pain and maintaining the pace in the remaining miles I was starting to get excited about the possibility of success.

It was just after twenty miles when I felt I was holding back just to stay with the group. I decided I needed to go quicker so increased my pace slightly. The next couple of miles saw me maintain this pace and when I got to twenty two I still felt there was more to give. I took the plunge and increased the pace again. By this time I was running on my own and loving every minute of it. When I got to twenty four miles I looked at my watch and realised that I was over four minutes ahead of schedule. It was at this point that I realised I was going to break three hours. With just two miles to go and me still running strong and feeling good there was no way I was going to let it slip. With this realisation a shiver went down my spine and a big smile appeared on my face. Luckily I was still running on my own, because if someone had been with me they would have wondered why I was running with a huge grin. This surge of adrenalin spurred me on even more, and I cruised across the finish line in 2.53.55. This meant I had done the second half of the race in under one twenty five, which was close to my best. I had not felt this emotional since my first marathon and was on a high for weeks after. I finished seventy fourth and was beside myself with excitement. I had finally smashed the barrier that had been in front of me for the last few years. The surge of confidence this gave me was hard to describe. I just wanted to tell everybody what I had achieved and how it made me feel. Sub three, the words were just magical to me. I was in the same hour as the world record holder. I had worked so hard to gain this and now I had it, all I could think of was could I go quicker. I can't explain how much of a lift this marathon had given me, suddenly all the tiredness and leg aches disappeared and training was a pleasure.

You would think this race would spur me on for months to come but after just a couple of weeks I started to question the result. Was the course short? Was the timing wrong? Was it just a freak result I would never repeat? All these questions went through my head as I pondered how to overcome this feeling.

I then decided that the only way to verify this event was to run another marathon as soon as possible. I looked at the calendar and picked out a marathon in Sasolburg which would take place on Saturday 23rd February. This was just four weeks after the Johnson Crane but I entered anyway. Looking back now I wonder what made me think that running two marathons in four weeks was a good thing and all because I could not believe how well I had done in the first one.

I continued with my normal training for three weeks and then in the final week I decided to have two days rest before the event. This sounds good but my best friend Bernie was leaving work that week so we all went out for a drink on the Thursday night, which was a big mistake. I stayed out drinking with Bernie and by the time I got home I was totally wrecked. It was only eight o'clock but I went straight to bed and only woke to be sick several times before the alarm went when it was time to get up for work on Friday. I managed to get to work but spent the whole day feeling sick. One of my work colleagues was also going to run at Sasolburg and he asked if I was still going to turn up. I told him I would only go if I felt better when I awoke on Saturday morning.

Saturday morning came and I felt a little better so decided to go along and see what would happen. I met my work colleague at the start and told him I was just going to take it easy and see how far I could get. The race started and as I expected I felt awful. For the first five miles I thought I was about vomit, I didn't and over the next few miles I gradually started to feel better. By ten miles I was going quite well so I upped the pace and the further I ran the better I felt. In the last ten miles I felt I was flying and stormed over the finish line in nineteenth position in a time of 2.50.30, another personal best. How do you explain a personal best over a marathon distance with a hangover? I could not work it out but I was elated and realised that my Johnson Crane time was no fluke as I had broken three hours again. I would now only look for quicker times and not worry about that three hour time, it had taken me quite a while to get over that particular hurdle, but now I was there I would no longer be looking back. I even went out the following day and ran a half marathon distance just to get the aches out of my legs.

Confidence restored I threw myself into my training with no real purpose or plan. I just wanted to race as much as I could while the high of my marathon success seemed to make running so much easier. I trained hard and managed to get my half marathon time down to one hour fifteen minutes and thirty seconds. This time was as significant one as it meant I had qualified for the South African championships. Unfortunately the championships were to take place in late July and I would not be around long enough to take part. Even though I knew I was due to leave South Africa I continued to race and train as normal. I even competed in a half marathon event the day before we were due to fly back to England. In fact I completed a total of 60 miles in that final week.

From the beginning of 1985 my personal circumstances were going through another big change. My time in South Africa was about to end. Our time there was a bit of a disaster. Lesley was desperately unhappy and the country was going through a period of significant change. This change was having an impact on the country's economy, and even though these changes were long overdue I felt nervous about committing my future to the country in these uncertain times. Riots had started in the townships in late 1984 and were even bigger than the 1976 riots. This continued into 1985 and I felt that the long overdue end of apartheid was closer than ever. I must admit I was nervous about how this change would come about and as I had a young family to think about I felt it would be better if we returned to England. It was many years before the apartheid regime was finally overthrown in early nineties but the country continued to experience dramatic changes throughout the eighties. This continued to have a negative effect on the economy and looking back I am glad I came home when I did.

Africa had given me so many good memories and improved my understanding of the very different cultures and lifestyles the world had to offer. I had been lucky enough to visit so many places in my lifetime. I had toured Europe twice, the first time for six weeks in 1974 and then for three months in 1979. I had travelled throughout Southern Africa during my time there and been to some fantastic locations. All the major cities, Johannesburg, Durban, Cape Town, Bloemfontein, Maseru, Mbabane, Harare, Maputo and Gaborone. I had been to spectacular places of interests such as the, Kruger National Park, the Wine Route and Table Mountain in the Cape, Rorke's Drift and Isandlwana in Zululand. I had driven across the Kalahari Desert en route to Cape Town. I had driven from Johannesburg to Harare in Zimbabwe then on to the Gorongosa National Park in Mozambique before returning to Johannesburg via Maputo and Swaziland. On another trip I drove from Johannesburg to Harare then on to Victoria Falls and back to Johannesburg. All in all I have memories of Africa that will live with me forever, but now my time here was coming to an end. I would return to visit on several occasions and I will always have fond, plus some not so fond, memories of my time there but for now my thoughts were on a return to England.

We finally put our house up for sale in January 1985 and it sold almost immediately. When we left in June we had to pay 2.2 Rand for every pound and even though we had not been there long, it gave us enough for a decent deposit on a house when we returned to the UK. By December 1985 you had to pay double that amount, and the Rand never really recovered from that position as it deteriorated year on year. I look back at the time we spent in South Africa and I am so grateful for what it gave me, precious time with my parents and relatives, a son and finally a real appetite for running.

We arrived back in the UK on eighth July. I felt I had really progressed with my running and looked forward to the forthcoming races in the UK. I did not realise how the pressure of finding work and somewhere to live while bringing up a child would affect my running. The times I had achieved in South Africa were very good and it was not long before I realised that trying to better them might not be possible as I was now approaching my mid-thirties and there were many other things to occupy me over the coming twelve months.

11 NOWHERE TO RUN

"I just run as hard as I can for 20 miles, and then race."
-Steve Jones

Before I left South Africa I had taken a look at the UK running calendar with a view to competing in a marathon as soon as possible after my return. I wanted to put the excellent training I had done towards achieving a marathon best, so I entered the Bristol Marathon which was taking place just six days after my return. In hindsight this was probably a bit too soon but I was confident I could do well. I started well but faded badly over the last six miles and finished, disappointed in 2.52.10. This was a measure of how far I had come in my running when a sub three would feel like a failure. Only six months earlier I was desperate for such a marathon time. Putting this failure behind me I took some time away from running and concentrated on finding work and a house. We were staying with my mother in law but were keen to find a place of our own. I managed to find work at a small engineering firm but this was not very secure and every few week's people were called into the office and given their marching orders. It was not the best environment for a settled life and my running definitely took a back seat during this period. I did not race again until September and in October, following a couple of races, I took some time out while a house move, work commitments and family life took over. It was December before I started to run again and as I looked back at a year that had started so positively I could not help feel that the one thing I was missing was being part of a club.

I had done all my training on my own since returning to the UK and this was having a negative effect on me both physically and mentally. The other problem was I was working all day and when I came home Lesley would go to work for a few hours while I looked after Lee. Then when she came home from work I would then go out for a run, which sometimes was as late as nine in the evening. I tried eating as soon as I got home but I just got indigestion and stomach pains when I ran. I then tried running and then eating but this meant I was eating between ten and eleven at night, which meant I did not sleep as well. I felt I was treading water and my running had become stale and matter of a fact. The only positive to all this was that I was still running and had not given up completely, because I believe now that if I had given up at that time I would probably have never returned to the sport.

1986 and 1987 were not much better as I tried to get myself settled and run again. I joined a local gym where I picked up with another couple of runners, so I started to get out a bit more. I even managed a marathon personal best at Gloucester in October 1986, where I finished in 2.49.11, and a 10k personal best in April 1987 with a 34.36 at Frenchay in Bristol. Even with these good times I still felt there was a lot more to come if only I could get myself fully motivated again. The time just drifted by without me really getting to grips with my training and I feel the real problem was finding the right incentive to train and improve. I was settled at home and I now had secure employment at British Aerospace so I had no distractions but I could not seem to find the drive and enthusiasm I had just before leaving South Africa. I needed a club atmosphere to motivate me and fellow club members to push me to train harder. I literally felt I had nowhere to run as I continued to do the majority of my training on my own. I lacked direction, structure and a willingness to push myself.

One significant event did occur over these quiet years, I managed to get a place in the London Marathon. I had tried to get entry into this prestigious event since I had started running, but it was almost impossible to get a place. What I did not realise was that the gym I was running from, The Empire Club, was also a registered running club, even though there were only about half a dozen people there who ran. This status entitled them to a single guaranteed entry into the London Marathon The guaranteed place normally went to those who had been there the longest but for the 1987 entry people were either injured or did not want to run, so it was passed down to me. The event lived up to expectations and I loved every minute of it. I did not get a great time I finished in just under three hours in an unremarkable run. What really stayed with me was the atmosphere surrounding the event. It was fantastic and to this day I still say to people "If you are only ever going to run one marathon, then make sure it's London". It is an unforgettable experience and the crowds are the ones who make it thus. They don't stop cheering you and it makes you feel as though you are out in the front of the race. I have now competed at London on nine occasions and have enjoyed every one, even if I had a bad run or conditions were not great I still thoroughly enjoyed the occasion. I think it is the whole build up that makes the race what it is and for years whenever I said I was a marathon runner the first thing that people would ask is "have you done London". Before I gained entry to the race this comment used to annoy me. It was almost as if you weren't a real marathon runner unless you had competed at London. I began to understand this once I was in the event, in the week before the race people at work would ask me for my race number so they could look out for me on the television. It is an event that captures the whole nation and for me has become the best marathon in the world, long may it continue.

1988 saw me knuckle down and put a lot more into my training. I started to run more often and I also joined a local running club, Great Western Runners. This was to be a turning point for me as I rediscovered the running club atmosphere and started to join in with track sessions, at Whitchurch Airport, as well as taking part in more races, including relay events where the club atmosphere was at its best. GWR had lots of talented runners and I was determined to try and compete with the best of them.

The coach at GWR for our track sessions was a guy named

Arthur Dagger. Arthur was a runner who ran for the pleasure. He was never concerned about how long it took to complete events he just loved to take part. He took part in many events for the club and was a stalwart at the Gwent league x country events. Sadly Arthur passed away suddenly in 2008 and GWR set up a memorial fund in his name. These words about Arthur are written on the GWR website: *"The Arthur Dagger Memorial Fund was set up in memory of Arthur Dagger who died in 2008. He was one of the longest standing members of Great Western Runners, a stalwart who had been on the club's committee for many years and who worked tirelessly for more than a quarter of a century on behalf of the running community in the Bristol area. He especially had a track record in supporting young people in their running. The Fund's Mission is to support young people in Avon to develop their talents and improve their competitive running."*

This says it all about Arthur. I had the pleasure of attending track sessions coached by Arthur for a numbers of years. It was during this period that I achieved all my best times and I can honestly say that he was the best track coach I have ever worked with. He would always be there, no matter what the weather. There were times in the winter months when the weather would be foul and about three people would turn up for the session, but Arthur would still be there and put the same drive and enthusiasm into the session as he did when we had ten or fifteen people. He also had the ability to know if you were slacking during the session. Even if there were ten of us doing 400m reps he would know what times we were all capable of and give us a shout if he felt we were not performing up to scratch. He knew when we were training for a big event and maybe we were a bit tired, his words of encouragement and his knowledge of running would mean he always got the best out of you. He was also a presence at races, again shouting words of encouragement when you least expected it.

It was on one such occasion that led me to my best time over 5k, when taking part in an annual series that took place in Bath city centre. It was an unusual event in that it was a very short loop around shops by the Cathedral, and to make it 5k you had to do seven and a half laps. It was during one of these events, when I was having a personal battle with a good friend of mine, Steve Crummock, that Arthur suddenly appeared. The race started as I expected, with Steve going off at a blistering pace and me struggling to stay with him. I knew it would settle down and as long as I kept him in sight all would be fine. True to form after a couple of laps I started to slowly gain on Steve, then, with two laps to go I went past him. Generally this would mean I would finish in front of him, but on this occasion Steve fought back and passed me with just half a lap to go. I felt I was going as hard as I could and would not be able to get back to him, but just as that thought crossed my mind Arthur appeared and shouted "Come on Bill you can catch him! Remember the track work". This really did galvanise me and I gave my all trying to catch Steve. Just a few yards from the line, much to his surprise, I passed him and crossed the line to finish in 15mins 59secs. This was the only time I ever broke sixteen minutes for 5k and I believe I have Arthur Dagger to thank for that. Steve's time was sixteen minutes dead and strangely enough it was the quickest he did while I knew him, he was absolutely gutted he did not manage to break sixteen minutes. So that was Arthur, a man I had the ultimate respect for and a man who, over the next few years, would help me to improve in all areas of my running. His track sessions were the backbone of my improvement then, and in later years later would prove invaluable to me in a different way.

So with all this going on I eventually started to see my running improve once again, even though it was near the end of the year before my efforts paid dividends as I bettered my marathon time with a 2.48.20 at Gloucester in October. My training was going well and by the end of the year I had done one thousand five hundred and fifty seven miles, which was the most I had done since my successful stint in South Africa in 1984 and 1985 where I clocked up one thousand nine hundred and ninety eight miles and two thousand and six miles respectively. All in all I was in a very positive frame of mind as my enthusiasm returned, and I felt that the next couple of years would give me the opportunity to achieve what I felt I was capable of. As long as I could stay injury and illness free.

12 PEAK TIMES

"The miracle isn't that I finished. The miracle is that I had the courage to start."
— John Bingham

1989 started with me in a very positive frame of mind. I felt fitter and stronger than ever and was determined to push myself and see what I was capable of. I was really beginning to understand about running long distances and started to adjust my training to include all the different elements I felt were needed for me to become as good as I could. We all have a level of ability and once you really become focussed on your training improvements start to happen. The next few years were to prove to be my most successful. I went from strength to strength and my race times started to really improve. I was working harder than ever and the improvements just kept coming. I had tinkered with my training plan and had gone back to running lots of shorter distances to improve my speed. I knew I had the endurance but I felt I just needed to get quicker, then I could add on the miles and see what happened.

This all worked out very well and over the next couple of years I clocked up more miles than I had ever done before and gained best times at all distances. The two times that I am most proud of were London Marathon 1990 in 2.35.40, and 1991 Stroud Half Marathon in 1.11.17. Everything was coming together and I really felt I could get better and better. How much quicker could I go? I threw myself into my training with even more determination and confidence. I now had a real knowledge about race preparation, when to rest, when to train hard and how to taper for important events.

While all this was going on I was also more settled in work and at home. I was starting to take on more senior roles at work and my lack of self confidence started to fade into the background. This was obviously aided by the success in my running. I was in a good club atmosphere and there was good healthy competition at all distances and everything was going well.

This first sign of things not quite going according to plan was at the start of 1991. I started my sixteen week marathon plan in January confident that I could better my London time from the previous year. Five weeks in and I started to get some Achilles pain. I had any easy week then pushed on again the following week and continued to train hard until I finally broke down in week ten. I immediately contacted a physiotherapist and was told I had Achilles Tendonitis. This meant complete rest so my dreams of London glory were out of the window. At the time I was not that upset, I would give myself time to recover and once I was running again I could target another marathon later in the year. I was given the all clear by the physiotherapist in the middle of April and started running again. I still had to do a lot of self massage and icing to do to the tendon, but soon got running again. Although I did not compete in another marathon that year I still managed to get that career best half marathon time at Stroud, so not a bad year.

I went into the next year full confidence of a marathon best at London. Again I started my sixteen week plan in January and this time managed to see it through to completion. The day of the race was mild, sunny and breezy so excellent marathon conditions. Unfortunately for me I did not quite run to my best on the day, and even though I did 2.36.28 I felt really disappointed that I could not improve on my previous best. My running diary says "A bit disappointed with this time. Never really felt comfortable during the race. My best spell was between ten and fifteen. Really started to hurt at sixteen and the last six were really painful. Cannot understand why I struggled, the pacing was good and the weather was good. Do I re-think my training strategy or just put it down to a bad day". Looking back at my diary it told me the reason I had felt 'not quite right' on the day. Five weeks prior to London I competed in a marathon race and although I tried to take it steady I pushed on in the last few miles and did 2.42.02. Then two weeks later I competed in a really tough twenty mile race in mid Wales. This just shows that sometimes, even when you think that you have mastered the art of training/racing you can still get carried away and do things completely wrong. If I had just done the marathon race or the Rhayader twenty then I am sure I would have been fine for London, but doing both was a step too far.

It may have been my undoing that year but the Rhayader 20 was a great event and I don't regret finding this little gem of a race. I was to return to compete in this race quite a few times and picked up quite a few prizes along the way. It was without doubt the toughest twenty mile event I have ever done but at the same time it was the most spectacular. If you have never been to the Elan Valley in mid Wales then you are missing something spectacular. The race started with three laps of the village, each lap containing a short steep climb followed by a short steep descent. This set the scene for the race and after three laps you head out of the village before turning right and heading north towards the reservoirs.

The Elan Valley Reservoirs are a chain of man-made lakes created from damming the Elan and Claerwen rivers within the Elan Valley in Mid Wales. The reservoirs, which were built by the Birmingham Corporation Water Department, provide clean drinking water for Birmingham in the West Midlands of England. The race winds its way around these reservoirs and does so with stunning results. I have run the event in all kinds of weather and it never fails to give me a great feeling of satisfaction upon completion. The views are always spectacular even when the elements are at their harshest. I have seen these reservoirs looking like a mirror in sunny windless conditions and have also seen them with waves on them as they are battered by ferocious winds.

After the right turn out of the village the road starts to climb and this climb goes on for three miles. It starts gently enough but there are sections that are exposed and steep. In my first run on this course these exposed sections had a major effect on the runners because we were running uphill, into a 30mph wind and then we had hailstones. Hailstones hurt enough without being driven by a 30mph wind. I was with a small group of runners at this point and tried to hide in the middle of the group to get a bit of protection but even then it was painful and it was very, very cold. We battled on through this for a couple of miles and finally reached the top of the climb. The wind was still strong but the hail had stopped. We then ran across the top and started the descent. As we reached the top of the descent the clouds dispersed and below us lay a wilderness of hills. I could see no roads except the one we were on. This was unlike any road race I had ever done, and despite the bad weather I was really enjoying it. From this point on the road undulated continuously as we threaded a course around the spectacular scenery of the reservoirs. The first flat section did not arrive until mile sixteen. By this time I was on my own and had not seen another runner for quite a few miles. There were one or two spectators but it was like doing a really tough solo training run. Just when I thought the course had flattened the sting in the tail arrived. Eighteen and a half miles in and there was another hill, not the longest or the steepest on the course, but it came at a point when my legs were just about finished. Luckily for me as I reached the start of the climb I saw someone walking ahead of me. This was what I needed to get a response from my tired legs. I pushed on and managed to overtake the runner and then it was the final one mile run back into the village. I crossed the line totally spent but had managed to secure a fifteenth place finish. I was exhausted and for days after my legs ached, my body was tired and I developed a sore throat and a bit of a cold. Looking back at my diary now it was obvious that I was not going to be able to perform at my best in London but at the time with my confidence and self belief on a high I could not see how wrong I had got it.

 The rest of that year went well and as I was still getting good times I went into 1993 with confidence and high hopes. My running diary at the start of the year said that my targets were 'close to 2.30 for marathon, sub 1.11 for half marathon and sub 54 minutes for 10 mile'. This shows I still had belief in my ability to improve even more. I think when you are in that place where good performances come continuously you can see no end to it and it takes a while of just missing out on best times before you realise that maybe your best is behind you.

This realisation does not stop the belief, it just takes a bit of time before you begin to accept it. Even then the drive to train and race hard stayed with me, my self confidence and self esteem had really been boosted by my running and my promotions at work. I was no longer that shy, self conscious individual. People in both of these environments were asking for my input and advice and seemed to genuinely respect what I had to say. This became more and more evident in my running, where I found myself offering advice to newer runners in the club. I felt I was in a good position to do this as I had made every mistake in the book and wanted to try and help these people to avoid those same mistakes. Even though I was still making some mistakes myself I felt I could offer some insight into the mysteries of this sport and enjoyed just talking about running and the ups and downs of racing.

The other elements of running that affect performance are simple things like clothing and footwear. For years I suffered with blisters between my toes and quite often finished a race with bloody socks. I tried different types of socks including twin skin and waterproof, I tried no socks, talcum powder and loads of Vaseline. Vaseline was the treatment I stuck with even though it was not one hundred percent effective. I was putting Vaseline on my feet for every run but the problem persisted right up until I started to do a lot more off road runs. Initially this made my feet worse but eventually the continuous wet feet and foot movement in the shoe actually started to harden my feet. Now I only put Vaseline on if I am going out for a few hours. I also tried lots of different types of shoe. What I discovered was I had narrow feet and a lot shoes just gave me too much movement until I found that Adidas were quite narrow so suited me. The transition to off road was even more painful. The main shoes when I started off road were Walsh's and they crippled me. Again I found the answer with Adidas Swoop shoes and then moved on to Inov8. All this trial and error is part of getting everything right and progressing as a runner.

The clothing issue I had was twofold, first it was the vests. I suffered runner's nipple on a couple of occasions and believe me getting in to a shower with runner's nipple is one very painful experience, but once again Vaseline was the answer. The running shorts of the time were also a major problem. They were call split leg shorts and were designed to give more freedom of movement. The only thing they did for me was give me an awful rash between my legs as the excess material gathered in that area. Again lubrication was the only thing I could do but I continued to suffer until, initially, lycra shorts were introduced and finally the longer leg shorts that are worn today. Even now I wear a pair of running boxers under my shorts and no longer have the problem. All these things are an issue when you start running and they have to be dealt with because the last thing you want to be worrying about when you are on the start line is whether you are going to be bleeding, blistered or chaffed by the time you get to the finish.

So I entered 1993 high in confidence and enthusiasm for the coming year. Targets were set and I was up for the challenge unaware that things were not going to go according to plan and that I had already hit my peak times.

13 WALK DON'T RUN

` Running is nothing more than a series of arguments between the part of your brain that wants to stop and the part that wants to keep going."
— *Unknown*

1994 started off like any other year, a review of the previous year along with target setting for the coming twelve months. I was quite positive about the coming year and setting targets always gave me focus. Unfortunately the knee pain I had been experiencing was getting worse. I saw a physiotherapist, who recommended a few weeks rest but that did not work so I went to my doctor and was told the same thing.

Lots of rest and not so much running through the year meant a very frustrating year. It was a very depressing year because I was injured but I continued to battle through with the hope that all would be ok. What is it with the running fraternity that makes us think that if we continue to run while injured it will eventually go away. I did this continually through this period even though I was running badly and was constantly in pain. My diary entries show I was consistently under achieving but still I continued. Being injured and running off and on was the story of the whole year and I will admit I was feeling a bit sorry for myself.

I gradually dropped away from the club scene and was a bit miffed when, apart from Arthur Dagger and people I regularly ran with, nobody from the club made contact to see how I was. After all I had been one of their most active runners since I joined in 1988. Why I thought anybody would be interested in my wellbeing I am not sure. The club and the runners all moved on and I was just part of their history.

. My training was all a bit half hearted and this was reflected in the notes from my diary at the end of the year "What a miserable year. No targets achieved, no personal best's set, the lowest yearly mileage since 1983 and dogged by injury and illness. My knees are still not right so it will be difficult to set targets for next year. I can only hope that 1995 will be better."

I tried running again in the early part of 1995 but soon broke down again. I also resorted to acupuncture to try and solve the problem but once again I was told to stop running. Early in the year I got to see a specialist who took x-rays and explained what the problem was. Apparently the problem started after I had my varicose veins done in June 1993. There was a six week recovery period followed by a couple of weeks of trying to run again followed by three weeks holiday in South Africa. After the South Africa trip I returned to the UK and raced in a half marathon just a week later. The only reason I took part in this event was because it was part of a series sponsored by Adidas and I was currently in third place. The race went ok, although I did drop a place to fourth, and afterwards I carried on training as though I had had no time off. This was the mistake. The small muscle groups around my knee were weak and my knee cap was moving about causing it to wear away underneath, hence the pain. I can even trace the moment back to when it started because I was so meticulous about keeping my diary. This is the entry the day after the half marathon. "A bit sore from yesterday, so this was a slow run. A little bit of pain in my right knee but otherwise I feel good." That was the moment, the start of all the problems but, like any other runner, I just carried on training and racing as if there was no problem. This problem stayed with me right up until I saw the specialist early in 1995.

So what was the diagnosis? Would I still be able run? The specialist basically told me that the damage to my knee cap was permanent and there was no fix, but with physiotherapy I would be able to run. How much and how far would be my decision because I would always have pain, it was just up to me to determine how much I could put up with. This was not the best news I have ever had but I decided on complete rest until my course of physiotherapy was complete. At that time I was always in pain, even when I was just walking about. The specialist assured me that with the right physiotherapy I would be relatively pain free but could not say how this would be once I started running again.

It was at this time that I started to do some walking. Initially it was short walks around Bristol but it soon developed into a desire to go further and higher. This is when I started to visit areas like the Brecon Beacons, Snowdonia, Scottish Highlands and finally the Lake District. I really developed a love of walking in the high fells and although initially my navigation was awful, I slowly started to improve and gradually my navigational skills improved to the point where I felt I was able to find my way on most terrain in good and bad conditions. The mountains I visited during this early spell left me wanting to do more and more. How could I resist such delights as Snowdon, Scafell Pike and Ben Nevis.

These were the highest but there were certain first time events and locations where I just wanted time to stand still so I could remain in the moment forever. Like the first time I drove into Glen Coe from Rannoch Moor and was awestruck by the sheer size and beauty of Buachaille Etive Mòr as it thrust skywards at the entrance to the valley. The rugged climbing face of Ben Nevis as I made my way along Carn Mor Dearg Arete. The knife edge ridge of Crib Goch towering over Llyn Llydaw and Glaslyn, on the ascent of Snowdon. The magical rock formations on the summit of Glyder Fawr and Glyder Fach in Snowdonia. The appearance of the mighty Helvellyn in the early morning sunshine, as I made my first ascent of Striding Edge.

These moments captured me and even when things went wrong or the weather was bad the hunger to explore these high places remained with me. It was the first time in my life that I was not taking part in sport so I suppose that walking was my substitute for this.

These hill adventures were to continue when I started to run again a few years later, but for now I was just walking not running. My passion for these areas of high mountains grew throughout this period but in particular my love of The Lake District was firmly entrenched. My first attempts at some of these walks, was a bit embarrassing as I continually misjudged terrain, weather and which direction we were actually walking. With a bit of reading and lots of practice I improved but not before I had made lots of errors. Fortunately none of these were catastrophic and I never had to call on Mountain Rescue during this learning period.

The Lake District holidays I started at this time were a joy and I have been there at least once a year since 1995. My favourite place in The Lakes is the Langdale Valley. On my first visit in 1995 I was awestruck by the beauty of the place, the lush green valley and the towering mountains that surround you as you drive in. Although I did not walk any of these high mountains on my first visit I would return the following year to attempt Crinkle Crags. I had chosen this walk because I had found an extract from one of Alfred Wainwright's famous books and decided this was to be my first major walk. It ended up as a typical Lake District day with early sunshine giving way to mist and drizzle on the summit followed by a clear sky by the time we got back to the car. In between we got a little wet, a little cold and a lot lost, but we also had some great views of the surrounding fells and valleys. This adventure made me even more determined to do more of this sort of thing and although this was a welcome distraction I still wanted to run so I kept up the physiotherapy in the hope I could get back out on the road doing what I loved.

It was five months before I ran again. My first run back was in June 1995. It was three miles and felt like thirty but I managed two more runs that week. From that point I started a slow and steady build up as I tried to regain some of my fitness. I also noticed at this time that my asthma seemed to be particularly bad. Normally I would take the preventative inhaler during the hay fever season with the occasional use of the emergency inhaler, but now I found I had to take the emergency inhaler before major efforts, and in the end I started to carry it with me on runs. After a visit to the doctor he suggested I should use the preventative inhaler year round, which I started to do, but that summer was a bad one for me and I suffered quite a few asthma attacks. Over the next couple of years this situation improved and I still take the preventative inhaler every day to combat the condition.

Later that year the knee pain returned and again I had to take some time out. This was very frustrating but the specialist had told me in the beginning that my running would depend upon my pain threshold. So once again after a couple of months break I returned to my training. It was now February 1996 and in terms of running I had gone through a pretty bad spell and was beginning despair about ever getting back to running regularly.

It was during this time of recovery that I bumped into an old running adversary, Dave Rexworthy. We had done battle in several races a few years earlier and we got chatting. He suggested I come along to his club, Bitton Road Runners, as I would probably know quite a few of the runners. At first I was a bit reluctant but eventually I went along and realised how much I had missed being in a club atmosphere again. I was regularly strapping my knees for runs and I was still suffering. Gradually as my strength and fitness returned I started to run without strapping and even started track sessions as well as slightly longer runs. I was running again but not at the level I wanted, it was a very frustrating period and I even contemplated giving up completely, but slowly my fitness started to return. The pain in my knees was easing and I was beginning to race again, albeit over shorter distances.

I gradually improved and towards the end of 1997 I decided to have another go at the marathon distance. I entered London and started my sixteen week programme in January 1998. It did not go too well initially as I struggled with the increase in mileage along with the quality. My diary was full of entries stating how tired I was and how much I was struggling to cope. At the end of January I entered a 10 mile race but dropped out at seven miles because I could not cope with the pace at the end of a tough week of training. This used to be bread and butter to me and I always took pride in my ability to push my body week in week out while doing high mileage and racing at the same time. Maybe that had all gone, was it too much for me, and could my body now cope with these high demands, because I was only going to do London if I could do myself justice. I knew I would never get back to the level I was five years ago, but I still felt I should be able to compete and enjoy my running again.

I persevered with my training through January and slowly felt my strength returning towards the end of February. I ran a hilly ten mile race at the beginning of March and managed to do fifty nine minutes so things were starting to look up. I also did a couple of 5K races in a reasonable time before making the journey back to Rhayader at the end of March. This event would tell me how fit I was and whether I had the strength to do myself justice in London. Conditions were perfect, overcast and cool, as we set off round the village. I had gone along with a couple of other Bitton runners to show them this wonderful race. I had told them about the three mile hill and it was definitely as tough as I had remembered. The top of the climb was the six mile mark and I was there in thirty eight minutes. A couple of runners went past me as we headed down the hill on the other side but from seven miles on nobody passed me and I picked up a few places to finish in eighth place in two hours and six minutes. I was really pleased with this result, I had run well, even if the hill at eighteen and a half nearly destroyed me again, and it gave me lots of confidence going in to my final weeks before London. At the end of the race we watched the prize giving and saw the large trophy that was handed over to the Team Winners. We all looked at this and felt that it would look really good in the trophy cabinet at Bitton. Could we assemble a team of four good enough to take this prize from Poole Runners, who had won the trophy over the past few years? We decided there and then that we were going to give it a try.

Over the remaining weeks up to London I ran a couple of shorter races but concentrated on my final training weeks with the hope of reaching the start line in good form. London that year was wet, windy and cold and a stark reminder of how tough marathons are. I was struggling to keep to my pace from the beginning, and although I had a good spell between fifteen and twenty one, the last five miles were pretty awful. Still I crossed the line in two hours forty nine minutes and fifty five seconds, not bad for a forty four year old who had dodgy knees and had not run a marathon since 1993.

Buoyed by this effort I threw myself into my training and did lots of shorter races, I also put in an entry for Dublin Marathon in October. I was getting decent times for my races but was beginning to see that, at forty five years of age I probably was not going to get back to my times of five years ago. I began to look at this as a new start and set my targets as best times for a veteran. October came and it was time for Dublin. The weekend away was great but the marathon itself was a bit of a disappointment. I never really got going and in sunny, cool but very windy conditions I just managed to get below three hours. There were lots of Americans in the race, most of them walking. The walking event started an hour before the runners so it meant in the second half of the race I was continually hearing "way to go!" shouted at me and my fellow marathon runners, from our American friends. I was really suffering in the latter part of the race and their encouragement did not really do anything for me, but I did appreciate their enthusiasm for this rallying call as they had nearly four thousand runners go past them.

I was running again and was managing the pain. It felt good and I was really enjoying the experience. I could not do as much as I used to and I was a bit slower but I was back and looking forward to new adventures in 1999. It turned out to be a year I will never forget, it had positives in terms of my running, but they were far outweighed by more personal tragedies.

14 3-HOWTOWN TO PATTERDALE

"Start slow, then taper off."
- Walt Stack

Running out of the checkpoint from Howtown I felt good. One more leg to go before I reached halfway, and a much needed break with lots of refreshments. Each competitor had a drop bag at the half way point and this bag could contain anything you wanted. My drop bag contained a complete change of kit. I had decided on the change of kit because I felt it would signify the end of one race and the start of another. When you have been running for hours in the heat and in the same kit a change just has a really positive effect on you. I never thought I would get beyond halfway and here I was planning to get fed, watered and changed before setting off on the second part of my Lakeland adventure. I felt I deserved some sort of reward, but there was still a lot of work, including Boredale Hause, to complete before I could feel too smug about what how I was doing.

It was during the run along the Boredale valley that I started to feel quite fatigued. I went through a spell where once again my confidence deserted me. I was beginning to tire quite dramatically and this was not helped by the fact that I could see all the way to the head of the valley, and it looked such a long, long way away. It was also around midday and the clear skies meant the sun was high and the temperature was rising, and until I reached the top of the Hause it was going to feel like running in an oven.

There was hardly a breath of wind as I made my way along the valley floor. It seemed to take an age to reach the beginning of the main climb and the heat became even more severe as I battled my way up to the top of the Hause. The start was gentle enough but I was soon walking as the climb became steeper and my legs tired more and more in the oppressive heat. The confidence I felt at Howtown was now gone as I struggled with the climb. I just kept telling myself "one foot in front of the other and you will get to the top". After all no climb goes on forever, even Mount Everest has a summit and no climb is infinite. These strange mind games are all part of running. There are lots of little tricks you have play with your mind no matter what distance you are running, it's a constant battle of mind over matter, and as a very good football coach used to shout at us "I don't mind and you don't f*!^&*g matter".

I kept my head down and tried to walk as quickly as possible, not looking up at how much climb I had left. I had used this method for big climbs quite a lot and found that it helped keep me going at a decent pace. The aim was to focus on the three or four metres in front of you and to just keep moving. By not looking too far ahead you had no idea how much more climb was in front of you and if it went well I would not look up until I felt the ground in front of me start to level out. I would occasionally look back, mainly so I could see how far I had come, but also to take in the wonderful Lakeland scenery. A blue sky and clear air meant everything was pin sharp. Weather like this was not the norm in the Lake District but when it occurred it was a joy to behold, the peaks that surrounded me were all clearly visible and the lush greens of the valley contrasted with the browns of the summits.

Boredale Hause is a steady incline but becomes very steep just before the top of the Hause is reached, so I knew I was near the top as the ground before me steepened. Still I kept my head down and soldiered on. Suddenly I heard a voice call out "well done you've reached the top, just a short run down to Patterdale now". I looked up and there just a few yards ahead of me was a course marshal. I don't think I have ever been so pleased to see someone in my entire life. I had made the top despite feeling down and out for most of the way. I thanked the marshal as I walked a few more yards across the top to a small cairn signifying the head of the Hause. There below me was the valley and the village of Patterdale. What a welcome sight this was as I managed to break into a run for the first time in what seemed an age. The track down to Patterdale is wide and easy going, I felt much more confident now as I descended to the half way point of the race. I was still desperately tired and in need of good refreshment but I knew I was going to continue and even felt quite excited about the adventure that lay before me.

As I reached the valley floor and made my way along the road to the field tent at the half way mark, any thought I had about catching Claire had now vanished. It was one thirty and the climb over Boredale had taken longer than I had anticipated as well as taking an awful lot out of me, which meant Claire now had a ninety minute head start on me. The way I felt at that time there was no way I was going to catch her. On the run in to the half way tent I was greeted by supporters and was very surprised to see quite a few runners in the tent. After I had collected my drop bag I sat myself down in a vacant chair, and took advantage of the very welcome relief from the sun that the tent provided.

Before the race I had set myself a target of a five minute stop at each checkpoint with a ten minute stop at halfway. This had not really worked as I was taking at least ten minutes at each, bar the first one, and I knew I was going to be in this tent for some time. I took a look around me at the other athletes and knew that some were dropping out. You could see it in their faces as they sat slumped on chairs and on the ground around me. I sat and contemplated this myself but despite the tiredness I was really beginning to enjoy the event. The weather was perfect and I felt, for the first time in the race, that I could actually make the finish in a reasonable time. So I sat and took in lots of food and drink while I changed into my clean, dry kit. This was definitely a good move, I just felt renewed by the feel of this fresh clothing, I was ready to take on the next part of this challenge and even though I was there a while I knew I was going to continue. I felt confident I could carry on without my body giving up on me. I finally left the tent to start the next leg of my journey in the knowledge that there were probably going to be many more miles of highs and lows in both terrain and emotions before this particular adventure reached its conclusion. With this thought in mind I set off along the road toward the Grisedale Valley.

Distance covered 30.3 miles
Time taken 7hrs 17mins 52secs
Overall position at Howtown 54th
Overall position at Patterdale 53rd

15   THE END OF AN ERA

"Life is short... running makes it seem longer."
- Baron Hansen

Two tragic things happened in 1999 and both were to affect me personally and both will be with me until my dying day. First my Mother passed away in July and then my Father passed away in November. What can I say other than it was devastating and it is something that I feel you never really get over. There is not a day goes by where I do not think of them and how they shaped me and loved me and supported me. I would give anything to be able to spend just one hour with them even now. What made it even more difficult was they were in South Africa so I could not just pop round when they were ill to see them.

In their later years Mum and Dad had turned to religion. When we lived in Chester Mum would send us to the Catholic Church and make sure we put some money on the collection plate. We were raised as Catholics but were never seriously religious, in fact once we moved away from Chester the church going activities stopped. The church they had joined was one of those that had large congregations and lots of singing. A small percentage of Dad's pension was given to this church every month. I did not have a problem with this, if it gave them comfort in their later years then that was fine by me. I will say that when they both died the church were brilliant, they took so much pressure off my sister Vicky, and the rest of us by organising the ceremony and the burials. I am not very religious but I will always be grateful to the church for the amount of effort they put in to make sure everything went as smooth as possible.

My youngest sister, Vicky, was still living in South Africa at the time, my other sister Pam was living in New Zealand and my older brother Allen was living a few miles from me, in Bristol. It was in the early part of the year when we had a call from Vicky saying Mum was not well and had been taken into hospital, shortly after she was in a coma. Vicky kept us informed of her condition and in June told us that she was riddled with cancer and the doctor's did not hold out much hope for her recovery. Pam had already been over from New Zealand to see her and Dad and now it was Allen and I who decided it was time to get over there.

When we arrived in South Africa and I first saw Dad I could not believe how small and frail he looked. I had not seen him for a few years but he looked totally different. His twice daily visits to Mum in hospital had taken its toll and I feared for his health. Maybe because I was not there to see them that often I would always see them as I remembered them from my childhood, as the strong characters who had protected, comforted and cared for me.

The next shock was on our first visit to the hospital, where Mum was hooked up to a machine that was keeping her alive. Once again the contrast to the person from my childhood was so stark. Mum had always been the life and soul of the party and was someone who never minced her words. If you had done something she did not approve of then she had no qualms about telling you. I remember as a teenager during my apprenticeship me and a couple of my friends started talking about leaving home and moving in to a flat together. I mentioned this to Mum and she said "that's fine but just remember when you move out and claim your independence you don't come back here for money, food or to get your washing and ironing done". I know this sounds harsh but she was just trying to make me understand the economics of what I was planning to do. When I sat down and really thought about it there was no way I could afford to move away from home while still on apprentice wages. Her comment just made me sit and think and of course I did not move out. When I told her I was not going she said nothing, she just came up and gave me a hug. When I left a few years later her and Dad gave me so much support organising my move back to England, and even put a few pounds in my bank account to help me on my way. This was Mum, hard as nails one minute and so supportive the next.

We had been in South Africa for a week when Allen had to leave to go back home. I had decided to stay another week. Mum's condition had not improved and the doctor's sat us down and spoke to us saying it was only a matter of time and that the only thing keeping her alive was the machine. This was devastating news and Dad was all over the place, they had married on 24th December 1949 so had been together for fifty years. He was not looking well and I was worried about his well being.

On one evening I convinced Dad he should stay at home and rest and I would go and visit Mum. This was the first time I had been there on my own and I sat and held her hand and spoke to her for the whole hour of the visit. I spoke about everything I could remember from my childhood, the funny incidents, the naughty incidents and I also apologised for some of things I had done that I knew had upset her. At the end I told her she was loved by many and that we would all miss her when she was gone. This talk with Mum was something I will never forget, it was just me and her, and I really do believe that she could hear me even though she was being kept alive by the machine. Mum passed away on 5th July 1999 and was just 68 years old.

Dad and I spoke a lot while I was there visiting, and after Mum had died I said to him "Dad, when all this is over you should to come over to England and stay with me for a while." I felt he needed a break and to be somewhere different.

Where Mum was the hard one Dad was more of a soft touch and seemed to accept what came at him without it seeming to bother him. Having said that he had moments when he would lose his temper but it was all over very quickly but you knew you had pushed him too far when those moments arrived. Dad was not one to show his emotions like Mum and sometimes it required her to tell us how hurt or upset he was by something we had done, because he would never show it. One such incident was when I borrowed his car one Sunday morning to drive to Johannesburg to play football. After the game I was driving home when a car came round a bend on the wrong side of the road and hit me head on. Thankfully nobody was seriously hurt but Dad's car was a write off. Me in my teenage ignorance just assumed that Dad would claim the money back through his insurance and would have another car in no time. It took a few weeks but eventually he had another car and although I had said sorry to him and he had said "that's ok it wasn't your fault", I thought that was the end of it. About a month later Mum came up to me and started having a real go at me about the car. I said I did not know what the problem was because Dad had another car and was ok about it. Apparently this was not the case, the car, a white Triumph 2000 with overdrive, was his pride and joy. She told me that he absolutely loved that car, and as for the insurance payout there was a five hundred rand excess which he had to pay. She was having a go at me because I had been so matter of fact about the incident and had not offered any money to Dad to help pay the excess or offered any help to get him a new car. I just stood there and said I thought everything was ok with Dad because he had said nothing."That's because he's your dad and he is too soft on you and does not want to say anything to upset you, but inside he is hurting". What Mum was really upset about was the fact that I had not offered any help at all. She told me that he would never had accepted any money from me but the least I could have done was drive him around so he could find a replacement instead other people had done this. It's amazing how selfish we can be when in our teens, something I am not proud of and was one of the things I apologised for in that talk by her hospital bedside. I know I must have disappointed my dad at times during my life but I am sure that in the end he was proud of me, as he was of all of his children and the life he had given them.

Sadly after I had returned to England his health deteriorated and, although I spoke to him regularly on the phone, I was never to see him alive again. When his condition got worse I booked another trip to South Africa and was due to fly from Heathrow Airport on 12th November. Pam was already there from New Zealand and on the 10th of November we got a call from her saying that Dad had died that morning at home he was 71 years old. She and Vicky were with him when he passed away. I still flew over on the Friday and stayed until just after he was buried alongside Mum.

    I was somewhat numb for quite some time after these events and I must admit it really does make you take a good look at yourself and your life. It was the end of an era but life goes on and you move along with it. I am blessed with loads of great memories from my childhood and I treasure each and every one of them. When we were younger and lived in Chester Mum and Dad always tried to take us out on day trips into North Wales. They enjoyed the outdoors so much and this continued when we moved to South Africa where they loved to travel to the Eastern Transvaal to enjoy the stunning mountain scenery of the Blyde River Canyon, God's Window, Mac Mac Pools, Lisbon Falls, Berlin Falls and Bourkes Luck Potholes. Their enjoyment of visiting such places certainly rubbed off on me and I am sure my love of the Lake District and other mountain regions is down to them, so thank you Mum and Dad.

    In my own life I try to enjoy something in every day, even when I have a bad day I try to find something in there for myself, something that makes me smile, something that brings back a good memory, something that makes me feel good inside. Sometimes it is something as simple as stopping to take in the surroundings, great views and scenes are often missed because we are so wrapped up in our own thoughts. Sometimes just doing something for someone else, even though it may be an inconvenience to you at the time, can bring a real a sense of well being afterwards. None of us know what tomorrow is going to bring so make sure you enjoy today.

16   HEAD FOR THE HILLS

"Anybody can be a runner. We were meant to move. We were meant to run. It's the easiest sport."
-Bill Rodgers

The one good thing that happened in 1999 was completing my first Mountain Marathon. While running with Bitton I became friends with Bryan Stadden and Dave Bulley. Bryan was responsible for introducing me to off road running and Dave became my main Mountain Marathon partner. Up to that point I had always been a road man, totally focussed on pace, race times and personal best's. I had done a few off road events and x-country races but did not imagine I would ever be a serious off roader. Bryan mentioned Mountain Marathons and like most people I assumed this meant running a marathon distance in the hills. Not so, a Mountain Marathon is usually a two day event where you have to visit controls in a mountain area. You have to carry enough kit to enable you to camp out in the hills overnight and for safety reasons you have to run in teams of two. The real skill in these events is navigating to reach all the controls. At this time there were three main events during the year. The LAMM, which was my particular favourite, was held in some remote part of the Scottish Highlands in the first or second week of June. The Saunders, which was always in the Lake District and took place in early July, and the KIMM which could be in any mountainous area in the country and was held on the weekend when the clocks went back at the end of October.

The first one I took part in was the LAMM. Once all entries have been accepted the venue was described as "*About 2 HOURS DRIVE NORTH OF GLASGOW/ EDINBURGH and 3 HOURS DRIVE WEST OF ABERDEEN. The exact location of the event will NOT be divulged to any competitor until 36 hours before the event*". This was different, all I knew was that I would be somewhere in Scotland. Thirty six hours before the event we learned that the event centre was located in a field by the Inveroran Hotel in the Blackmount area. This was at Loch Tulla just north of the Bridge of Orchy. I was now going to put my walking navigational skills to use in a running event and started reading the event information. What was I to make of such instructions as, *"Maps will be handed out (2 per team) a few minutes before you start. Maps are not waterproof so please ensure that you take a suitable map bag with you and in the event of bad weather we suggest that you save one map for use on the second day. The six figure grid references you will be given, represent the bottom left corner of a 100m square. The exact location could be anywhere within the 100m square and the description should enable you to locate the checkpoint precisely. Due to the steepness of the ground, some checkpoints will be described as being, for example, 'on the 540m map contour'. This is to enable you to locate the precise point on the map and it may not always accurately reflect the height you are seeing on your wrist altimeter (should you be lucky enough to have one)!"* And *"Please be prepared for the worst possible conditions as the competition area is very isolated and these hills are exposed to serious weather. Bear in mind that you are very much on your own once you have started. Although the organisers will ensure that the event is as safe as possible, your safety is ultimately your own personal responsibility, just as it is with any trip into the hills. Consider training for this event by running on mountain terrain where possible and by practising fine map reading and compass skills."* Then *"Each person must wear or carry a whistle, compass, map, pencil & paper, torch (not penlight) with spare bulb & 6 hours light, sleeping bag, survival bag (not space blanket), waterproof cagoule with hood, over trousers, hat & gloves, tracksters/thermal bottoms, thermal vest or similar, warm thicker top, hill food for each day with a small amount of emergency rations to remain at the end of day 2."* And last but not least *"FORBIDDEN KIT: GPS and any Satellite Navigation device such as Magellan - altimeters are allowed."* Well if I was not nervous before I was certainly a very worried man now.

The other issue that was worrying me was my feet. I had always suffered with blisters even when running on a flat surface so how would I cope with two days of running on uneven mountainous terrain and in possibly wet conditions. I would just have to make sure my navigation took me through the best of the terrain and would try and keep my feet dry as long as possible.

We travelled up to Scotland on Friday and in the car was myself, Dave Bulley, Bryan Stadden and his running partner Andy Creber. It was a long drive from Bristol and once out of the car we headed over to the main field to pitch our Friday night tent. The idea was to have a larger tent and warmer sleeping bag for Friday evening so we could pack our rucksacks including tents ready for the off on Saturday morning. Once the tents were up we had a walk over to the marquee to register and get our start times for the morning. As this was my first one, myself and Dave had entered the 'D' class, while the more experienced pair of Bryan and Andy were in the 'B' class. This meant they would have more distance to cover and probably more technical controls.

People were arriving continually through to late evening and by the time we climbed into our sleeping bags the field was full with around five hundred teams. The site of all these tents in a field in the middle of nowhere is quite spectacular and over the years of doing these events I never tired of the buzz and the excitement that was so prevalent on the Friday evening. The only thing that usually detracted from this was the midges. That first event was bad but not the worst, Glenfinnan in 2008 holds that title. The event centre was right beneath the famous Harry Potter viaduct that year and the midges were horrendous. Standing at the start waiting for the instruction to go I still had waterproof leggings, long sleeved top and midge net over my head. I only took these items off about thirty seconds before the off and even then I had to stand there swatting the midges with my map.

Going back to that first event, Myself and Dave got ourselves ready and walked to the assembly point at our allotted time. On the previous evening there had been lots of chatter about the area and about which direction we would be heading out. I soon learned that in the LAMM this was a pointless exercise. Once we had assembled we were loaded on to buses and driven 10 miles to the north. This event always had something different and that's why I loved it so much. During my thirteen outings in the LAMM the Saturday morning start was always well away from the event centre. On the walk to the assembly point we were handed our two maps but would not receive our grid references and control descriptions until we started the race. The bus took us north towards Glencoe but then turned off left and headed along a very narrow road into Glen Etive. After a couple of miles the bus stopped and we were all dropped at the side of the road. We were surrounded by big climbs and unless we were going to run along the road it was going to be a tough start. The area was full of teams heading to their various start points with marshals shouting which direction to go. 'D' class was called and the marshal shouted "Make your way over to the marshals on the side of the hill across the other side of the road", the only problem was that between us and the start area was the River Etive. We crossed the road and before us was a scene of chaos as hundreds of runners waded through fast flowing waist deep water just to get to the start line. That put to bed any thoughts of me keeping my feet dry for as long as I could. We made our way down to the river bank where we found ropes that had been placed at intervals to help us get across the river. We took the plunge and emerged on the far bank soaking wet from the waist down. A short walk up the far bank and the various courses were then funnelled in to their areas.

Before we had time to think about how wet or cold we were our start time was called. We made our way forward into the 'D' class funnel and stood nervously on the start line. Finally the call was given out "Go!". There was then a brief five metre run to the next area where we collected our control descriptions and then we had find a spot to read the controls and mark them on the map. This is a really important part of the race, getting those controls marked in the right place takes time, but nowhere as much time as it would cost if you marked any one of them in the wrong place. Controls marked and we were off, on a big climb and over to the next valley towards our first control. That first day on my first Mountain Marathon was hell, my navigation was not great, too many wrong route choices, and within the first hour I could feel the blisters starting. We did eventually make it to mid camp after six hours and forty one minutes out in the hills, one hour and forty five minutes behind the leaders and in twenty fourth place. Even through all the pain the environment and the views were fantastic. We even had a control on the summit of a Munro, Stob Coir an Albannaich. During this ascent we had to climb through a snow filled gulley, this is what Scotland had to offer in June.

The terrain was tough and unforgiving, especially if you made bad route choices like me. At the top of the Munro I had a look at the map and decided to drop down into a valley to get to our next control, thinking that it would be level running on the valley floor. Bad decision, getting down to the valley floor was a battle over rocks and through heather and once down there it was so boggy any progress was slow and painful. The better route would have been to stay high and make use of the tracks that tended to run between Munro's in the Scottish Highlands. This error probably cost us half an hour but was all part of the learning.

It had not been a great day and my feet were bleeding and badly blistered. We met up with Bryan and Andy and they were in second place just four minutes behind the leaders. This meant they would be in the chasing start on Sunday morning. In these events if you finished within a certain time of the leaders then you would set off at that time behind them on Sunday. You also had a position number pinned to your rucksack and this created a great race environment. The rest of the field only started once all the chasing start teams had departed. We exchanged stories about our first day exploits and I then showed them the state of my feet and said I was not sure if I would be able to run on them in the morning. They then produced the magical 'surgical tape'. This white tape was very adhesive and they taped each of my toes individually as well as wrapping my feet completely in it. I had my doubts about how this would work but I would find out as soon as we got going in the morning.

After a fairly uncomfortable night's sleep we were woken abruptly at 6am. This was also a LAMM tradition, as someone dressed in the full highland kit would walk around mid camp playing the bagpipes to awaken the competitors on Sunday morning. First thing was breakfast, cup of tea and then toilet. What can I say about toilets on the LAMM, they were just another thing that made this event what it was. Basically just away from the main camping area six foot deep slit trenches were dug, one for the ladies and one for the gents. These were about two foot wide and separated by some wind breaks. Toilet rolls were scattered around the sides and you had to pick one up on your way in before deciding whether to go 'face to face' or 'face to arse'. Whichever way you chose it was not a very pleasant experience. When the trenches were fresh upon arrival on Saturday they were bearable, but by the time you came to use them on Sunday morning after a few hundred competitors had used them it was a bit of an ordeal to say the least.

For those of us not in the chasing start we had a little more time to ready ourselves so myself and Dave went along to see Bryan and Andy as they set off in the 'B' class chasing start just four minutes behind the leaders. After they had departed we packed up all our gear and made our way to the mass start. The control descriptions were available about thirty minutes before the mass start so our map was already marked up and ready. It was overcast with drizzle as we lined up with a few hundred other teams and then we were off. This second day was much better, my feet held up with all the surgical tape, and navigationally we were a lot better. We were the third team home on Sunday just eight minutes behind the leaders and finished our first event in twelfth place one hour forty minutes behind the winners. Bryan and Andy overtook the leaders and finished in first place in the 'B' class.

So that was my introduction to running in the mountains and I loved it. I had done a couple of single day events in South Wales but this was something else and I couldn't wait for the next one. I had gained important navigational experience and now had the magic tape for my feet, what could go wrong? As we had entered the KIMM in October I would soon have the answer to that question. This was to prove to be a completely different animal and showed me how tough and unpredictable these events could really be.

17 A STEP IN THE RIGHT DIRECTION

"If you don't have answers to your problems after a four-hour run, you ain't getting them."
— Christopher McDougall

With my first mountain marathon in the bag I returned to the roads for the summer, but after a couple of months the knee pain was so severe I had to take a few weeks off. I started running again in early September with the aim of getting fit for the KIMM at the end of October, so by the time the event arrived I had about six weeks of running behind me.

The event was to be held in Scotland on the Cowal Peninsula in Argyll. The forecast for the weekend was pretty grim but the journey up on Friday was fine. Dave and I had entered the 'B' class and set off on a wet and windy Saturday morning. The weather throughout that day was horrendous and in these conditions we struggled to find some of the controls. I can even recall crawling across a narrow section on my hands and knees, because of the wind, to reach a control. We had been out in these conditions for nine hours and still had three controls to locate when we decided we had had enough. It took us another hour to get to the mid camp on the edge of Loch Eck and when we got there it was dark. We then had to find a decent place to pitch the tent in a field that was just a bog and after walking around for half an hour we managed to find a small spot that was not too flooded. By the time we had organised ourselves and the tent it was nearly ten o'clock, it was pouring with rain and the wind was howling through the campsite like a freight train. These conditions persisted throughout a very cold and uncomfortable night. Needless to say we did not get too much sleep, and just to add to the discomfort the clocks went back so we had an extra hour to enjoy the cold wet tent.

Sunday morning could not come soon enough and as we were out of the race we packed away all our gear and set off towards the event centre in Ardentinny as early as possible. The only problem was that Loch Eck lay between us and Ardentinny. This meant we would have to circumnavigate the loch to get back to the event centre, which was a run of thirteen miles. The weather was marginally better but it was still pretty bad. We later discovered that over fifty percent of the 'B' class had dropped out on Day 1. After being out over four hours we finally arrived at the event centre. The scene that greeted us was one of devastation. Only about twenty tents remained standing in the field, the rest had been flattened. The organisers had gathered up as much as they could and put them all in a container in a corner of the field. Thankfully ours was one of the tents that remained standing so we were able to change into clean, dry and warm clothes. I cannot imagine what it would have been like if you had completed two tough, wet and cold days in the mountains only to come back and find all your belongings piled into an open, damp container along with loads of other clothing and tents.

This event showed me how much I still had to learn, handling the conditions and the terrain had proved our downfall. We were hoping our next one would be a more positive experience and sat down with Bryan and Andy later that year to map out the events we would go for next year. In the meantime I was determined to get more experience running over rough and mountainous terrain. Into the diary went the Dursley Dozen, Rhayader 20, the Black Mountain Roundabout, The Grizzly and the Welsh 1000's. All these events were great tests in their own right and would help me prepare for the four mountain marathons I had entered for this year. The GL3D at the end of April, the LAMM in June, the Saunders in July followed by another go at the KIMM in October.

It was setting out to be a really tough year and a very tough start to my training. I needed to get plenty of miles in before all these major events kicked in. I struggled through January but started to feel a bit better towards the end of February. The Dursley Dozen was really tough, very muddy, but I did ok. Rhayader 20 was once again very tough but satisfying because I was in the top ten and Bitton picked up the team prize, just holding off Poole Runners. Grizzly was next and this was even tougher, four miles of running along a pebble beach just about finished me off and it took all my strength and willpower to get to the finish line.

Next event was into the real mountains over in South Wales for the Black Mountain Roundabout. Twenty five miles starting in Crickhowell at 100mtrs elevation and then climbing up to Crug Mawr at 550mtrs. From there it is a run of four miles over a wet boggy ridge to Pen Y Gadair Fawr at 800mtrs and then to Waun Fach at 811mtrs. Then you lose nearly all that height you have gained to cross the road at Pengenffordd before climbing back up to Mynydd Troed at 609mtrs. The route then drops another couple of hundred meters before climbing back up to summit Mynydd Langorse at 508mtrs. There follows one last drop of about 300mtrs down to road level before the torturous climb up to Pen-Allt Mawr at 719mtrs. The last couple of miles takes you back to Crickhowell via Pen Cerrig-calch and Table Mountain. This is about six hours of very demanding terrain as it is always in April. I use this event as early year training for other mountain races. It is actually an event put on by the LDWA (Long Distance Walkers Association) so most of the entrants are walking but there are always a few runners who take part. With a good deal of snow at higher elevations this proved to be a tough day out and I was well pleased with how this went.

It was now just two weeks until the GL3D and I felt as ready as I could be. This event was over the Bank Holiday weekend and our start was in the village of Bampton on the eastern side of the Lake District. It was organised by Joe Faulkner and his aim was, in his words "The route was billed as 3 x 25 mile days and very much linear so that it is a large ranging tour of The Lakes. The routes changed every year, and we only release the day's route on the evening before. Another key GL3D factor was allowing runners to start when they wanted, rather than generate a list of start times; this lessens the stress factor as you can't be late for your start. We aimed to keep our overnight campsites very simple and remote, with limited vehicle access just for the baggage van, and have discouraged 'support teams'. Baggage was limited to a one hundred-litre Dry bag weighing no more than 12kg. We also always aimed to have a start/finish on the edge of The Lakes, and so keep entrants cars out of the Lake District National Park and basically adopt a green eco policy." I ran in four or five of these events and through this got to visit all areas of this wonderful National Park. It took me to areas that I would probably not have ever seen and I will always be grateful for that.

I really suffered on that first event, the distances involved and sheer scale of the mountains we had to climb was like nothing I had ever done before. I started the first day with Bryan and Andy and after eight hours in the mountains my legs had gone and I was just following. I did no navigation at all and had relied on Andy initially and then Bryan to get me to the finish line in Hesket Newmarket. This was because Andy had dropped out due to severe cramp. It was something Andy suffered a lot with when I first met him and it was quite a few years before he managed to get control of the condition. That day was overcast but it was very mild. The major climbs were Sheffield Pike, Blencathra and High Pike.

Andy had dropped out on the first day so on the second day I hung on to Bryan as best I could. I think he could have left me at any time as I was really struggling, we were out for over seven hours and I could hardly walk after five, but Bryan stayed with me to our finish camp at the northern tip of Thirlmere Lake. The last part of this day took us along the ridge from High Seat to Ullscarf. This is probably the wettest, boggiest ridge in the Lake District where running becomes an absolute nightmare. I was trailing Bryan by about fifty metres and every now and again he would disappear into a dip before appearing again on the other side. I soon learnt that each one of these dips was down into the peat bogs. It felt like this torture would never end but Bryan just kept forging ahead as strong as always, halting on occasion to let me catch up. We reached the overnight camp at Steel End Farm exhausted. Bryan had selflessly dragged me through two days of the toughest mountain terrain and I don't think I would have made it without him.

The final day was to be slightly shorter and I had decided to go out on my own so I would not hold Bryan back. I needed to do this so that I was getting the whole experience myself instead of just following Bryan. I needed to prove to myself that I could navigate my way through these mountains at a reasonable pace. I was quite nervous as I had never done anything on this scale on my own. The tough start took us over Seat Sandal and then on to Thornthwaite Beacon before the final high point of High Street. I was slower but I really enjoyed the day, no navigational errors and after six hours in glorious weather I hobbled into Bampton a very weary but very satisfied athlete. Three continuous days over these mountains and I felt I could tackle anything. True the weather had been kind but that did not lessen the challenge, and the final day on my own was an unforgettable experience, especially when I reached High Street, because I knew I was on the final ridge and not too far from the finish.

Having completed this event my sights were firmly set on the LAMM in June, just one more mountain race before I did this, The Welsh 1000's. Another event recommended by Bryan which started at sea level in Abergwyngregyn in North Wales. The race takes you over the summits of Carnedd Llewelyn and Carnedd Dafydd before a fantastic descent to Ogwyn Valley. Then the climb to Bwlch Tryfan and down to Pen-y-Pass Youth Hostel, then up again to the summit of Garnedd Ugain to finish on Yr Wyddfa (Snowdon), at 1,085m.

Bryan, Dave and myself were starting at Abergwyngregyn while Andy was doing the shorter route starting in the Ogwen Valley. By the time we were approaching Carnedd Dafydd Bryan started to pull away from me and Dave. We had decided to stick together as training for our upcoming mountain marathons. The weather had started to close in by the time we had reached Ogwyn and when we arrived at Pen-y-Pass it was raining heavily. Dave started to really struggle as we were climbing the Pyg Track. We had run out of food and it was still a long way before the finish. The weather was getting worse and as well as the torrential rain we were starting to get cold. Dave was so desperate for nourishment he picked a partly eaten banana from the side of the track and wolfed it down. This helped him a little but it was a long, cold, wet trudge up through the rocks of the Pyg Track to Bwlch Glas. This is where the Pyg Track joins the Llanberis Path up to the summit of Snowdon. At this point cold, wet and very tired, we had to turn away from the summit to get to the summit of Garnedd Ugain which is about twenty minutes of running in the opposite direction.

We reached the trig point on Garnedd Ugain and turned to make the final ascent to Snowdon. As we turned I looked at Dave and he was not in a good place, we desperately needed warmth and nourishment and we still had about thirty minutes of running before we reached the haven of the summit cafe, but Dave battled on and we finally completed the course in just over six hours, Bryan and Andy were there waiting for us. Once in the cafe we warmed up a bit and finally got some food. Dave was still looking pretty bad and as the finish line was on the summit of Snowdon, we still had to get back down to the car which was in Llanberis. Dave was quite weak and his lips were beginning to turn blue so we decided to put him on the train down to Llanberis. It took us a while to come up with enough money between us, and from very generous people on the summit, to put Dave on the train. We left him in the cafe and started our trip down the Llanberis Path.

It is quite amazing how the body can recover from such an epic challenge. Six hours of running in the mountains, an hour recovery and we were on our way back down to Llanberis. The rain had stopped and although at first it was painful, the leg muscles had tightened up and we were still quite cold, I was amazed at how comfortable the descent was. As we made this descent we noticed that no trains had passed us so Dave was still on the summit. We arrived at Llanberis after about an hour of gentle running and still no train had made the descent. We waited for a while and finally a train pulled in at the station and Dave climbed out of the carriage only looking slightly better. He told us how the wait seemed to last an age and he was getting colder and feeling worse. The journey on the train was no better because these things don't have heating and he was suffering even more. In hindsight it may have been better to take Dave with us, at least he would have gained body heat from running. What a start to the new millennium six months in and lots of races completed lots of mountains climbed but still plenty left to do.

18 CLIMB EVERY MOUNTAIN

"If you start to feel good during an ultra, don't worry, you will get over it."
- Gene Thibeault

The LAMM 2000 was to take place in Glen Shiel, the event centre was on the shores of Loch Duich at Shiel Bridge. Some five hundred teams converged on the event centre throughout Friday, we arrived late afternoon after a long drive from Bristol. Others had come by train, some had flown to Inverness then hire car and one team even arrived by helicopter. Once again the organisers had come up with a fantastic location. It was quite remote with some stunning scenery and an area of special interest to me, as I had booked a cottage holiday in the village Arnisdale later in the year. The setting for the event centre was quite something with views down the length of Loch Duich in front of us then the Five Sisters of Kintail stretching along the valley behind us.

I was really excited by the remoteness and the sheer scale of the area and could not wait to get started. On Saturday some classes were bussed off to another location, but for me and Dave our 'D' class start was a twenty minute walk from the event centre on a small spur close to our first climb of the day. The weather was fine as we collected our control descriptions and marked our maps. We started with a control at a stream source on the east side of A' Mhuing, this was within two kilometres of our start and was not too difficult to locate. It was then onto to the top of a Munro, Sgurr na Sgine, some five kilometres away and at a height of 946m. Then it was a two kilometres of nice grassy ridge down to a path/stream junction at 320m. From there we dropped into a valley at 250m before climbing up to a col at 480m approximately four and a half kilometres away. At that point we had done four controls and had just two more before mid camp. The next one was a stream bend in an area littered with streams. It was just two kilometres away at 400m height and we managed to locate this with no trouble. We then had the final control, which lead us into the mid camp. We finished in third place just under thirty minutes behind the leaders and were out for four hours and fifty six minutes which meant we would be in the chasing start for the first time.

After setting up the tent and getting some food and a hot drink inside us we sat down to have a look at the map and discuss how we felt it had gone. I then realised we were camped less than a kilometre away from the cottage I was renting for a week later in the year in Arnisdale. So we took walk out and went over to have a look. The road that leads into Arnisdale is a dead end road. It is about twenty miles from Shiel Bridge and the road finishes in Arnisdale. The village has a small store which was also the post office but that's it. It sits on the shores of Loch Hourn and opposite the Knoydart Peninsula, a spectacular area I was to visit a few years later.

We met up with Bryan and Andy at mid camp, or should I say we met up with Bryan. Andy retired to their tent upon arrival at camp and did not come out again until it was time to set off in the morning. The old problem with cramp had hit him again and the only thing he could do was rest. Andy and Bryan were in tenth place in the 'A' class.

The traditional bagpipe awakening greeted us at 6am and outside it was raining. We had our breakfast, paid a visit to the slit trench, packed our gear and nervously made our way to the start. The rain had stopped by the time we assembled with the other chasing start runners and we set off nearly thirty minutes behind our lead team and just over thirty minutes ahead of the mass start. Our first control was on a platform on the side of the hill in front of us. This entailed sixteen minutes of climbing and we were the fastest 'D' team to this control. As we looked back down from this control we could see the mass start gathering, hundreds of teams were assembled below us and would be swarming up this hillside within the next ten to fifteen minutes. Our next control was some three and a half kilometres away at the foot of a waterfall and we chose to continue to climb to gain the ridge path. After our very quick start I began to tire and really struggled for the rest of the day. We hit the controls alright but we were just slower than the teams around us. We were out for four hours and six minutes, ninth team on the day and dropped to fourth overall. We were a bit disappointed with that day's performance but fourth overall meant we were in the prizes and with over one hundred and twenty teams starting and ninety seven completing the two days, this was a pretty good result. Bryan and Andy finished eighth on day two and ninth overall in 'A' class. This result had given us great confidence for the forthcoming Saunders mountain marathon, which was just two weeks away and was starting in my favourite valley Langdale.

Just when you think you are getting the hang of these mountain marathons along comes one to bring you back down to earth. The Saunders 2000 was such an event. The event centre was Stool End Farm and our first control was a sheepfold at 350m two kilometres into Mickleden. For some reason I thought it would be a good idea to gain the height early and then contour along to the sheepfold. Big mistake, the going was rough and up and down and rocky. While down in the valley floor there was a perfectly good track that could have taken us below the sheepfold and it would have been a straight run up to it. This probably cost us about twenty minutes just on that control. Next were off up to Rossett Pike and a small pond near the summit, this went much better although it was really starting to warm up by now. It looked as though we were in for a clear, sunny and very warm day out in the mountains. Control three was at a stream source just above Mart Crag which entailed a run over towards Stakes Pass and then round the other side towards Pike O' Stickle. From here we had two kilometres of boggy ground to a pond close to Mere Beck. More boggy ground was awaiting us as we made our way to the middle of a marsh close to Sergeant's Crag and then a tough section as we had to get across to the Ullscarf Ridge and head for sheepfold on Watendlath Fell. From there it was straight down to a gate in a wall before hitting mid camp at Watendlath.

Despite our bad start we had managed twenty second place but we were over an hour behind the leaders. Mid camp was in a field beside Watendlath Tarn which was our bath on that very warm evening. We woke the next morning after a night of rain to a completely different day. The mist had descended and you could see no more than twenty metres away. Today was going to be a completely different challenge. The first two controls went fine and although we could not see anything we had hit them both spot on. The next control was where it all went horribly wrong. My route choice was good enough, from High Saddle we had to get to a sheepfold on the southern side of Easedale tarn, a distance of about four kilometres. The plan was to run over Ullscarf over to Greenhow Crags and then pick up the path that goes down towards Grasmere Common before turning off right below Stenners Crag and across to Easedale Tarn and up to the Sheepfold. Sounds simple enough, but unfortunately we came off Greenhow Crags too soon and ended up in Greenburn Bottom. This was one valley too far over and it was sometime before we realised our mistake. We should have noticed that we could no longer hear voices around us in the mist but we continued to descend and it was only when we were out of the mist and in the valley that we realised our mistake. This meant we had to climb up to Gibson Knott and rather than descend into another valley we ran down over Helm Crag, cut right and made the ascent of the main Easedale Tarn path. All this cost us an hour and although we made no further errors we ended up taking longer on the second day than we did on the first. This gave us a final position of forty eighth and again made me question my ability to navigate in tricky weather conditions.

There was now quite a long wait until the KIMM in the Lake District in October so once again I returned to the road and competed in plenty of shorter distance races culminating in the

Bristol half marathon at the beginning of October where I managed a very satisfying one hour and twenty one minutes. I had still been doing off road runs during this time, especially along the Cotswold Way, to keep the off road fitness levels up. These runs were slower but a lot longer than my road runs.

Dave and myself had decided to enter the medium score class in the KIMM, we felt that might suit us better because it was all about hitting as many controls as possible in a set time. This meant if we missed one we were not out of the race, we would just move on to the next. In the medium score you had six hours on the first day and five hours on the second. Two Points were deducted for every minute you went over these times so it was important to judge times and distances accurately. Unfortunately this proved to be our undoing as due to bad weather the river crossing we plotted at the end of the first day was not possible and we had to detour along the river to locate a bridge. We arrived at mid camp over half an hour late which cost us sixty four points, a third of our total for the day. The disappointment of the point deduction was made even worse when we found out that when we were assembled at the start it was announced that the particular river crossing we were planning would not be possible because the river level was so high and the stepping stones to get across were two foot under fast flowing water. Obviously we had been busy talking and not listening to the announcements, another valuable lesson learnt. The second day was a little bit better but we still managed to get back ten minutes late at a cost of twenty points. Our final position was 105th from 250 starters and 192 finishers. Not a great result but the KIMM was always very tough, the days were short and generally very wet mainly due to the time of year the event was held.

So the new millennium had started with me spending lots more time in the mountains, in both events and holidays, and I was very keen to continue with this over the coming years. We all met up again at the end of the year to plan next year's events but then foot and mouth came along. The first case of the disease to be detected was at Cheale Meats abattoir in Little Warley, Essex on 19 February 2001 on pigs from Buckinghamshire and the Isle of Wight. Over the next four days, several more cases were announced in Essex.

On 24 February, a case was announced in Highampton in Devon. Later in the week, North Wales was affected. By the beginning of March, the disease had spread to Cornwall, southern Scotland and the Lake District where it took a particularly strong hold.

By 16 March, the number of cases was at 240. By the end of March the disease was at its height, with up to 50 new cases a day. The effort to prevent the spread of the disease, which caused a complete ban of the sale of British pigs, sheep and cattle until the disease was confirmed eradicated, concentrated on a cull and then by burning all animals located near an infected farm. The complete halt on movement of livestock, cull, and extensive measures to prevent humans carrying the disease on their boots and clothing from one site to another, brought the disease under control during the summer. From May to September, about five cases per day were reported. The final case was reported on Whygill Head Farm near Appleby in Cumbria on 30 September. Whole areas of the British countryside were out of bounds, although we did manage to compete in the GL3D before the Lake District was shut down.

The prospect of no mountain events taking place in the UK countryside meant we opted for an adventure abroad and entered Euro KIMM. The event was held just outside Grenoble and was all score class, to be honest the abiding memory of the event was getting a bit of altitude sickness on the first day as we went over a very high pass. It was very different to UK events due to the fact that we were in the Alps and you had to stick to recognised tracks. You could not try and cut corners or take direct lines because the terrain was too steep and rough. The area had magnificent scenery and included running through two foot of snow when we went over the pass and the mid camp had a huge bonfire, music and beer. It certainly was an experience but I think I prefer the UK events where route choice can make such a huge difference during the race. Four of us went along to this event, Bryan with Andy, and myself with Dave. As usual Bryan and Andy picked up a prize and the whole weekend was a great experience. On the Friday when we arrived we walked into the village where we were staying to try and get a drink and food only to find that everything was closed and that the village only really came to life when the ski season started. We did manage to find one establishment open and duly consumed a decent amount of alcohol before staggering back to our tents. The post race food was exceptional and we were made to feel very welcome at the prize giving.

With 2000 being a year of many, many mountains and 2001 a bit of a anti climax I decided to throw myself into the world of Mountain Marathons over the next few years, competing in nearly thirty different events between 2002 and 2012. I had four different partners during my time in these events but the majority were done with Dave, a few with Nick Thorpe and a couple with Bryan. All different characters, Nick I knew from work and was a very determined runner, Dave was mister nice guy and never got angry about anything and Bryan was jus relentless on tough terrain. I ran with Bryan at the LAMM in 2012 and he destroyed me. I just could not live with the pace he set and he ended up carrying my rucksack for me on the second day, but he did drag me to the first veteran prize in the 'B' class, which was the highest level I completed in a mountain marathon.

The fourth person I partnered was someone I did not even know when I started out doing events in the mountains and I did not compete with this person until the Saunders in 2006. We went on to compete in ten mountain marathons together, the last one we did was in 2014. The events leading up to me partnering this person were life changing for both of us. The other thing was that I found a renewed energy in my training and running and really started to get excited about my running again.

19 4-PATTERDALE TO DUNMAIL

"Any idiot can run, but it takes a special kind of idiot to run a marathon."
-Unknown

After nearly half an hour at the half way checkpoint, I finally forced myself out of the tent to continue the race. I had taken on food and drink as well as a complete change of kit. Plenty of people were sitting with me and the longer I spent in there the more reluctant I was to continue. I could tell that quite a few were dropping out, you could see it in their faces, and sitting with them was not good, it was time to continue. As I left the security of the tent the sun was high in the sky, and it looked as though the glorious weather was set to continue. It took my aching body a while to get going but gradually I forced myself into a run and was soon making my way along a tarmac track to the head of Grisedale Valley.

I did not particularly enjoy these tarmac sections, probably because I felt I should be able to run them at a decent pace, the reality was that each little rise felt like a mountain and I occasionally had to walk. I could see a couple of competitors further ahead of me but as I looked back there was no one behind me. The other thing about running in a valley was you tended to be sheltered from any cooling breeze and this meant the heat was intensified. The tarmac track eventually gave way to a rough track that would lead me up to Grisedale Tarn. Grisedale Tarn sits at the southern end of the Helvellyn ridge between Dollywaggon Pike and Fairfield.

This was another familiar part of the Lake District as I had walked and run the Helvellyn ridge on many occasions as part of training or in Mountain Marathons. The climb from the head of the valley past Ruthwaite Lodge is about three kilometres and in the midday heat it really was a tough test both mentally and physically. My energy levels had been restored by the long break at the checkpoint and my foot pain had eased, but when I got moving again the pain in my knee returned and I noticed it was a bit swollen. The long haul up to Grisedale Tarn sapped my energy and by the time I got to Ruthwaite Lodge I was struggling, but I was determined to push on as I was gaining on a group of runners ahead of me. Once again I adopted the 'don't look up' method for the climb, passing the group and eventually making it to the tarn. With Dollywaggon Pike on my right, Fairfield on my left and fantastic views back down the valley, I paused a moment to take it all in. It was now mid afternoon and the weather was holding, so no relief from the hot sun. The track then went round to the left hand side of the tarn before the start of the long tricky decent to Dunmail.

I had done this decent before but I don't think I had ever felt as weary as I did at this point. It's a very technical decent but if you get it right you can descend fairly rapidly. Today I was doing this on very tired legs and the big step downs over the rocks become very painful. This was compounded by the pain in my knee, making it very difficult to throw myself into the downhill and steep rocky steps. I cursed, swore and stumbled down this track knowing that it was only just over a kilometre to the bottom where refreshments awaited me. Despite all the cursing and swearing I made decent time on this section but then lost my way a bit when I reached the bottom. I reached the road before I realised that I must have missed a marker. I looked back up the hill but could see nothing over the ferns. Hot and weary I started to make way back up the lower slopes looking for any signs of a marker to guide me. As I reached the part where it begins to steepen another competitor came down the hill. He was across the other side of a gulley to me but I told him that this was not the way. From his slightly higher position he managed to spot a small red flag which was over on his side of the gulley. I made my way across in his direction and tried to follow him to the checkpoint.

This slight error had only cost me about ten minutes in

time but had cost me a lot in terms of effort, energy and mental strength. The annoying thing was that I was only about half a mile from the checkpoint. I trailed into the checkpoint behind the runner who had come off the hill behind me feeling very tired and a little bit angry with myself.

When things like this happen in an event, it very easy to let it ruin your race as it dominates all your thoughts and energy. The only thing you can do is to try and forget about it and focus what's in front of you. There's no point in worrying about something that has happened, you can't change it and it will only distract you from what's ahead. I reached the checkpoint and spoke to the marshals and told them I felt the marker was not clear enough as I had missed it and ended up by the road. I was not surprised when they told me a few other competitors had also missed this marker.

While taking on some food and drink the other competitor told me this was the end of the road for him. He felt he had put everything into this race but was disappointed by how it was working out. I had seen him coming off the hill and he looked fine but obviously he felt he was underperforming. I tried to talk to him about how well he was doing, but he was adamant, and mentioned that he had been up with the leaders over the first couple of legs and felt that the only way he was going was backwards. He was a good deal younger than me and his decision shocked me a bit but I could understand how he felt. I had done a few events that had started well but ended with me getting slower and slower and in the end dropping out. Once again the temptation to call it a day came into my head. I was tired and if someone half my age felt it was too much then there would be no shame in me dropping out. I knew the only way to conquer this feeling was to get going again as soon as possible and put all those thoughts to the back of my mind.

I was hoping to go out from this checkpoint with the young lad who I had come in with but that was now a non starter. There were no other runners at this checkpoint but I had noticed a few runners leaving as I had arrived, so I decided to set off and see if I could catch them. The amazing thing about events such as this is the highs and lows. One minute I was thinking about dropping out and the next minute I setting off in pursuit of runners ahead of me. Things like this are difficult to explain but you just go with it and get the best experience you can from the event.

With the good wishes of the marshals and the lad who had dropped out I crossed the main A591 to start the next leg of this epic journey. It was a short run along the road on the western side of Thirlmere Lake before turning west and heading up onto a ridge, of which Alfred Wainwright had said he would not take his worst enemy.

Distance covered 36.5 miles
Time taken 9hrs 29mins 35secs
Overall position at Patterdale 53rd
Overall position at Dunmail 48th

BILL GRAHAM

Overleigh X-Country Team 1967, I am front centre

Overleigh Football Team 1968, I am back centre

RUNNING ON TIRED LEGS

Comrades 1984 with John McGowan

London 1998

Rhayader Team Prize, Me, Bryan Stadden,
Chris Jeanes & Julian Pontin

RUNNING ON TIRED LEGS

Saunders Lakeland Mountain Marathon 2007 with Claire

Joss Naylor Challenge, arriving at Kirkstone Pass

20 RUNNING ON TIRED LEGS

"Run when you can, walk if you have to, crawl if you must; just never give up."
 -Dean Karnazes

In January 2005 I walked out of my marriage to Lesley. It was the hardest decision I have ever had to make in my life. I knew people would be hurt but I was desperately unhappy and felt I just had to do it. We had been married for nearly twenty five years and doing what I did took a lot of soul searching on my part. Lesley had said to me that I had changed after my parents died. Maybe I had but I believe that I was unhappy before that and we had been going through the motions and we were together only because it was easy, familiar and comfortable. Making a move like that was very scary, I spent the first couple of weeks lodging with my brother and then I contacted an old friend and work mate, Dave James. Dave had split from his wife quite a few years earlier but still had the family home which was a four bedroom property in Downend Bristol. His son was still living at home and he also had a work mate lodging with him. He had a small single bedroom that was available and said I could pay my first month's rent by decorating the bedroom.

I stayed with Dave for about six months before I got a call from big Ian, who I had first met in South Africa, saying he had split from his wife and did I want to look for accommodation that we could share. We moved into a flat in Downend, two oldies who had known each other since the early seventies now sharing a flat felt like a scene from the Odd Couple. There were times during those first six months when I wondered if I had done the right thing. The hardest thing was telling Lee, I don't think he really took it in at first but it really hurt me to have to tell him. It's strange that even though I really wanted this to happen I was all over the place after I had walked out. Running and being part of a club really helped me through those difficult months. People at the club knew what had happened and I got lots of invites to go out for runs and any social events that were going on. I really do not know how I would have coped If I had not had Bitton Road Runners to focus on.

Because I was getting invited along to lots of runs my weekly mileage was increasing. Through February and March I was running about ten times a week, lots of miles, lots of quality and twice a day runs three times a week meant I was running on tired legs but my fitness level was increasing. There was quite a group of us going out on regular runs and we decided to test ourselves on something different. There was a thirty mile event being held at Oldbury near Bristol at the end of January. I suggested that the group should go along and use it as a very long training run. The plan was that we would all run together at a pace that was comfortable to us all. A few were a bit apprehensive but I assured them that the pace would be controlled and that they would all be fine. This race itself went really well, we ran at a pace we could talk and we even played a couple of guessing games to take our mind off the distance we were running. It was so successful that by half way a few other athletes had joined the Bitton 'bus' to help get them through the race. The weather was kind to us and those who took part were pleasantly surprised at how comfortable they had felt at this distance. We even managed to pick up a couple of age category prizes.

I went on to run lots of races in 2005 both on and off road including the London Marathon, Chester Half Marathon, Palma Half Marathon (dressed as a clown) and Rhayader 20 on the road. While off road I did the Black Mountain Roundabout, The Rhayader Mountain Trail, Cotswold Way Relay, the SLMM, the Longmynnd Hike and the KIMM. I also took part in the Castle Coombe Duathlon series through the summer. By the end of the year I had clocked up my highest yearly mileage since 1992 and was really enjoying my running again. I had learnt that with the right training I was still capable of enjoying my running and was doing some pretty decent times. Still quite a long way off my best but I was now over fifty years old so the slowing down was understandable.

The other major event that took place in 2005 was me meeting someone from the club who would a few years later become my second wife, Claire. We first spoke to each other at a club social event in late August and she told me she was having marriage problems and was not happy at all. I related what had happened to me and told her if she ever needed someone to talk to then just give me a call. We spoke a few times on the phone and met up for a coffee a few weeks later. I then went on a holiday I had booked a year earlier with my ex wife and my son and when I returned Claire told me she had told her husband it was all over. From my own experience I knew how difficult that must have been and I told her that if she ever wanted to go out for a run then to just let me know and I would make myself available.

I found that Claire was someone I felt comfortable with and I could talk to about anything and found we had lots in common. We started to spend quite a bit of time together both running and social and she became my fourth mountain marathon partner at the SLMM in 2006 and my wife in 2009.

It was around this time that I started to do more and more coaching. I had always passed on advice to other runners and had even started to set track sessions based on what I had done with Arthur Dagger all those years earlier, but due to latest guidelines the club had to provide licensed coaches for insurance purposes.

The club paid for a few of us to attend a one day England Athletics course which would give us level one cover. I went on to do level two along with Claire and one or two others to give the club a better coaching base. At one point we had around a dozen licensed coaches at the club but some were coaches by name and were not really contributing towards the coached sessions. I approached the club chairman at the time, Gordon Robbins, and asked that he make me a Head Coach so I could try to organise the coaching team we had at the club. I felt that as the club had paid for their coaching badges then they all needed to be involved in a common approach to coaching within the club. He agreed and we started to have coaches meetings to discuss how we could best serve the two hundred and fifty or so members the club currently had. This proved to be quite difficult at first and I think some of the reluctance was due to the fact that a few of the coaches were not that confident about taking groups. Once we assured everybody that there would be guidelines and regular coaches meetings to discuss issues and progress it started to work quite well.

One of the schemes we set up was mentoring whereby athletes at the club could be 'mentored' by a coach as part of their preparation for a particular event. This proved to be very successful and numerous personal bests were gained by mentored athletes. The first step in this mentoring process was a one to one session between coach and athlete. The coach would spend up to an hour talking to the athlete to gain some knowledge of their background. How long had they been running, what were their recent race times, how often were they running, what could they commit to in their preparation, what medical ailments did the coach need to be aware of, what were their ambitions and targets. All this information is vital if you are to give an athlete sound guidance. All athletes are different and most people you coach at club level will probably be no more than good club runners, but does that matter. No it doesn't, your job as a coach is to make sure you assist that athlete in becoming as good as they can be. We can't all be a Mo Farrah because we are all different and you should never compare yourself to another athlete. The only person you can compare yourself to is you. Am I doing myself justice, have I reached a level where I can honestly say this is as good as I am going to be. Unfortunately you won't know you have reached your pinnacle until you are past it. Then one day it will suddenly dawn on you that you are probably past your best. This is no reason to give up or have regrets, just move on and look at the next chapter in your running story.

I myself mentored an array of athletes from sub three hour marathoners down to a fifty nine year old lady who joined the club to start running for fitness. Her name was Pat Harley and I was speaking to her about her progress. She told me she would love to break thirty minutes in one of our local five kilometre races. She had done this race a few times and was regularly finishing in last place. I set her a plan and spoke to her about her running, trying my best to instil some confidence. Then in January 2008 I ran with her at the 5k where she achieved a time of twenty nine minutes and forty five seconds and not only did she not finish last she was second female over fifty five. I don't think I have ever seen someone as happy as she was with this result. For me, that is what coaching is all about, helping people to be as good as they can be, no matter what level they are, just seeing them improve and gain belief in their own abilities.

Part of this is getting them to listen to their own bodies and getting them to recognise the signs of over training and also under training. Having been through all this myself I knew what it felt like even though sometimes you cannot see the mistakes you have made until a race highlights them. Getting runners to do less is just as difficult as getting them to do more. I recall one particular runner saying they had done very little training one week because their legs felt tired. I knew this runner had a habit of doing too little so I suggested to them that sometimes you have to run through the tiredness to progress, and if you stop running every time your legs feel tired then how are you ever going to get the best out of your marathon race. I explained that at some point during that race your legs are going to feel tired and if all you have ever done on tired legs is stop then you are probably going to do that in your race. I believe it takes a few years of running to really understand what your limits are and getting to that point usually means a few failures on the way.

On the other hand doing too much is also a recipe for disaster and I have certainly experienced that as well. At one point in my training when I was at my peak I pushed the running on tired legs theory to breaking point. I was in the middle of my London marathon training and was averaging eighty miles a week. On this particular day I ran to work, about eight miles, then got the bus home, ran four miles from home to the track where I did a track session, then I ran four miles home. About two miles from home I started to feel weak and a bit dizzy. I slowed down and just about made it to my front door where I just sat down. I came out in a cold sweat and could not move for about twenty minutes. I eventually got to my feet and staggered into the house where I collapsed on the bed feeling awful. After another half an hour, in which time I took on food and drink, I managed to get myself showered and into bed and slept through until six the following morning. I was supposed to run about fifteen miles over the next couple of days but took both days off and returned feeling much refreshed, in fact I felt quite invigorated even though I felt guilty about having two days off. This did show me that having time off in the middle of a heavy training schedule is not a bad thing and sometimes is a necessity. People sometimes fret too much about missing training and try to 'catch up' in the following days. As long as it is only a couple of sessions, forget it, move on and continue your schedule as planned and forget about what you have missed.

The thing to remember is that we are all different and respond differently to the pressures of hard training. I also believe that we all have the ability to reach a certain level in any sport. Too many people look at others and wish they could be as fast as them, but we are all different, and even if I was to train the same as Mo Farrah, there's no way I would be the same athlete as him.

Take the example of the club runner who trains poorly but is still one of the quickest in the club. In the eyes of the rest of the club this athlete is considered to be at a good standard, even though they don't appear to train properly. They either do too much training or not enough. People look at this person and say "They don't use a training plan and look how quick they are". This measure is purely based on the speed of the person who is making the comment. Put this same athlete in a county level environment and the comment would probably be "They could be a lot quicker if they trained properly". Put them at national level and they may be seen as a below average athlete who does not know how to get the best out of themselves. So when somebody says to me "They don't use a training plan and look how quick they are", I look at that athlete and see a person who has a certain level of ability, either physical or mental, which usually exceeds that of the person making the comment, and my reply is "just think how good they could be if they trained properly".

I am a firm believer in planning for an event and believe I have always had the ability to reach my peak for the target event. While on the subject of coaching I will say that I only got into coaching because of the track sessions I was taking and the insurance implications, although once I started the process I was very keen to progress. I attended lots of England Athletics coaching days as well as being part of the South West of England coaching improvement program. Unfortunately it took me a while to realise that the South West regional rep was not quite what he initially appeared. Promises were made but in the end I left the scheme because I felt he was only interested in his own progression and not of the coaches in the scheme. His way of keeping us on board was to flourish equipment and clothing at us to try and impress, but the one thing I wanted more than anything was for him to follow up on his promise of us all being 'mentored' by an international coach in our given discipline. After three years this failed to materialise but I had a nice new camera, some coaching manuals and the promise of an England Athletics coaching outfit for myself. Would any of this help me improve as a coach, sadly not, so I left the scheme feeling very disillusioned.

There also appeared to be a lot of snobbery in the coaching world, so much so that the South West rep wanted us all to have at least two regional class athletes against our names. This was obviously to show that he was doing a good job. Don't get me wrong, some of the coaches I spoke too were fascinating people but for me too many of them liked to 'name drop' the top athletes they had handled. I can honestly say that at a couple of the one day sessions I attended some of the talks went way over my head. It was more like a science lesson than a coaching course. My belief is that if you are talking to an audience then you need to have an idea what they hope to gain from you, and not just spout a lot of mumbo jumbo just so you can show everybody the extent of your knowledge.

Let me put it another way. How do you measure who is a good coach? Is it an international coach who has several excellent athletes under his wing and is measured on who he is coaching not what he has achieved. Or is it the club coach who takes someone who has not run since their school days, is now middle aged and overweight, and takes them through to completing their first marathon within twelve months. I think I know which task is the more difficult. I know that there are a lot of good coaches out there that get lost in all the hierarchy and posturing that goes along with a system that I feel is missing the hidden gems that exist at grassroots level. There, with that little rant about coaching and England Athletics out of the way, where do I go from here. Older, slower and looking for new ventures, the mountain marathons were something I would continue but what else?

21 STRONGER FOR LONGER

"This means that I don't have to run faster than the psychotic-maniac-vampire-cannibal, I just have to run faster than whoever is with me when the psychotic-maniac-vampire-cannibal starts chasing us."
— Jim Benton

I had dipped my toe into the turbulent waters of ultra marathons when I had trained for Comrades in 1984 and the mountain marathons had given me experience of time on my feet for lots of hours, so maybe it was time to merge the two and take a look at ultras, both on and off road. I had already done a couple of things that had told me I was more than capable and I felt this could add an extra dimension to my running.

In June 2000 I had done a charity event at work in the main Brabazon Hangar at Filton, Bristol. They set up a treadmill on the hangar floor and I was to run as far as I could in a day. The day did not get off to a great start because the treadmill did not arrive until 10.30 and I was supposed to start at 8.00. I was to spend the day running on the treadmill with two buckets in front of me for people to throw in their donations. I must admit I had not realised how disorientating continuous running on a treadmill could be. The plan was to take five minute break every hour and each time I stepped off the machine I was more than a little unsteady on my feet. I had set myself a target of completing a double marathon by 5pm but with the treadmill delay this was going to be a tough ask. The task was made just about impossible when in the early afternoon there was a fire drill and we were all sent out of the hangar for thirty minutes. I continued to run for six and a half hours and covered forty four miles, eight short of my target. I don't think I could have gone any further because of two things. The first was that by the end nearly everybody had gone home so my motivation was gone and I was a very, very tired runner who realistically could run no more. We counted out the money the following morning and found we had collected nearly six hundred pounds.

My next venture into ultras was in 2003 when Bryan, Andy and myself entered the Longmynd Hike. The start was in Church Stretton in Shropshire and the distance was fifty miles over a mixture of road and trails. There were sixteen checkpoints and you had to self navigate and hit all the checkpoints in order within twenty four hours. It was always held at the beginning of October and the start time was 1pm, this meant that you had about six hours before it got dark. Once it was dark you had to team up with at least two other people, you were not allowed to continue on your own. Prior knowledge of the area was definitely a bonus. Unfortunately we had no knowledge of the area whatsoever. This did not affect me that year because I only made it to checkpoint eight at Bank Farm. I got there and the light was beginning to go so I had to wait to team up with two other people, but after waiting there for twenty minutes my enthusiasm had deserted me, and I dropped out. This race becomes a real mental battle when you reach the checkpoint where you have to stop due to lack of light. The marshals tell you that you have to group with two others, which is alright if you know the people at that checkpoint, but if you don't know them then you have no clue as to whether they will hold you up or you will hold them up. The aim is to get as far into the course as possible before this point because once you are running in the dark your pace drops quite dramatically. It also helps if you can group with athletes who know the course, as navigation in the dark is another level of navigation, as we were to find out in our next adventure.

In January 2003 Bryan had spotted the High Peak Marathon in the calendar, but we were too late because the event was already full. This must be worth doing if it fills up two months before the event. Determined to give it a go we made sure our entry form was in good and early for 2004. The team consisted of Bryan, Nick, Andy and myself. We all had plenty of mountain marathon experience so were fairly confident of getting round. We had set ourselves a target of twelve hours to complete the course, this being based on previous year's results, and the hope of reasonable weather and of course, no navigational errors.

A brief description of the High Peak Marathon is *'A 42 mile navigational challenge for teams of 4 around the whole of the Derwent watershed in the Peak District'*. Two things ensured this would be an extreme challenge. First it is run in the first week of March, when the weather was very unpredictable, and second is the start time. Teams set off at one-minute intervals starting at 11pm on the Friday night, so the majority of the event is in the dark.

Andy had done some research into previous events and the winners were taking about ten hours. He did mention one section in particular where the distance between two checkpoints was just 1km but teams were taking anything from thirty five minutes to one hour and twenty minutes to cover the distance. This should have given us some insight into the nature of the terrain.

Our allotted start time was 11.10pm, which was right behind two teams from GWR, my former club. We set off from Edale village in cool and misty conditions and soon caught the two GWR teams who were running together. We stayed with them as we negotiated our first climb but slowly we started to pull away from them. After thirty minutes of climbing Bryan shouted to Andy "How far is the checkpoint Andy, we seem to have been climbing a long time". "The next checkpoint is about 1km away," replied Andy. "What do you mean the next checkpoint, what about the first one" shouted Bryan. "We passed that one way back down the hill, didn't you see it" answered Andy. This all came as a bit of a shock because I was carrying the checkpoint 'dibber' and nobody had mentioned the first checkpoint. After a fair amount of cursing and swearing the only thing we could do was trudge back down the hill the get to the checkpoint. By the time we had done this all the other teams had passed us and we were now well and truly alone on the hill.

There was absolute silence as we re-grouped to decide what to do next. The majority of the teams were now about an hour ahead of us. After a few minutes discussing if we should go back to the start we decided that we had given everybody enough of a start and set off in pursuit. It was only after the event that we learnt that the GWR teams had seen us pass by the checkpoint but had said nothing, and I guess if the tables were turned we would have done the same thing.

It was at least another two hours into the event before we saw any other teams but by then we were moving well and confident of picking off a few more before the finish. During the first four hours the terrain was much as we had expected and good progress was made. The weather had deteriorated a bit and we were in quite a heavy fog. We had to remove our head torches because in mist the light shines straight back into your eyes. Instead we had to hold them in our hands and point them directly at the ground in front of us. The next four hours of the course proved to be the most difficult. We found ourselves in an endless peat bog, progress was very slow and I honestly thought were never going to get running again. We seemed to be either climbing into or out of these peat hags or trying to negotiate our way round the worst of the bog. During this section we did the awful 1km section, which took us about forty five minutes. It was during this section that Bryan disappeared up to his chest in the bog, it took the three of us to haul him out and he was seriously cold. Fortunately he had spare gloves to help get his hands warmed up but we had to push on as quickly as possible to get his body warmed up again. If it hadn't been a team event we would have probably used his head as a stepping-stone.

We only emerged from the worst of the bog once the sun started to rise. We reached a checkpoint where tea, coffee and malt loaf were in abundance so we consumed as much of this as we could in five minutes before we set off feeling refreshed and confident. The first couple of hours after this saw us making good progress but it was a very weary group that reached Edale after being out for twelve hours and forty minutes. We were placed fourteenth from forty teams (Only twenty seven teams finished the course), which wasn't bad considering we had given everybody a head start. We were fifth veteran team and managed to finish ahead of both GWR teams. It certainly was an experience but not one I think I would like to repeat.

Later that year I had my second attempt at the Longmynnd Hike but once again I dropped out before I started the section in the dark. I had reached one checkpoint further than the year before but still lacked the determination to continue. Maybe I did not have the mental toughness that was required to compete in this event. I seemed to manage when running with others but was struggling to cope when I was running on my own. Was this just down to lack of mental toughness or was it the way I was running in these events.

A few months after this failure was when I did the Oldbury 30, again it was a success but I was running with a group. I decided to give the Longmynnd Hike one last go, so in October 2005 I stood on the start line with Ian Hoare from Bitton. Bryan was injured so could not go but when we got to the start I saw that Joe Faulkner was there. We got talking about the GL3D and other events and he told us he was from this area and had done this event on lots of occasions.

My target was to get to the same checkpoint as the previous year before we had to group up. After about an hour of running I found myself on my own but I was going strong, I had left Ian and Joe behind and pushed on to the target checkpoint at Shelve thinking that I may manage to get one beyond this If I kept up this pace. Unfortunately a navigational error on the way to Shelve cost me about half an hour. As I arrived at shelve a group of three runners were just leaving and I knew them and they were a really strong group. I was cursing my navigational error because I knew I could have been with that group. I sat there for about ten minutes taking a hot drink and some food when Ian and Joe arrived. This perked me up because this was perfect, Joe knew the route and Ian was a good runner. After another ten minutes we set off in the dark. Joe's knowledge of the route proved invaluable and although we struggled at times, we made the finish line after eleven hours and thirteen minutes. I had finally conquered this race and found out that I was in seventh place before my navigational error. My finish position was fifteenth and I felt confident that I could do well in future ultras. I believe I had come to understand how to approach these races. Unlike marathons and lesser distances, ultras are so much more about mental toughness. In a marathon if you walk you are usually finished, there is no way back, but in an ultra you are probably going to walk at some stage or even stop and have a break. The trick is to tell yourself that this is part of the race and everybody else is probably doing the same, apart from the front runners. If you walk in a marathon it is because you are defeated but in an ultra it is part of your race plan. Build it in to your pre race visualisation. If you are going to walk make it a determined purposeful walk and not a 'that's it I'm done' walk. What you have to instil in your mentality is that every step you take, in the right direction, is a step closer to the finish so just keep putting one foot in front of the other and you will reach the finish line. It took me a while to understand that nearly everything I had learnt for road running was of no use for me when running an ultra. The two things are completely different and require a totally different approach, but more of that later.

2006 was a year of road running and mentoring, especially with Claire. Our relationship was blossoming and we spent a lot of time running together. I did London in two hours and fifty minutes and was running really well over all distances. I was caught up in all the usual road races and club team events, along with mountain marathons, so really did not have the time to fit in an ultra. I did look ahead to 2007 and decided that my next ultra was going to be something completely different.

22 INTO THE HOT SEAT

"If God invented marathons to keep people from doing anything more stupid, the triathlon must have taken Him completely by surprise."
- P. Z. Pearce

The next ultra I did was something I had looked at a couple of years earlier in 2005 but had to abandon at the last minute due to lack of support. The support in question was a lap counter and timer. This was a pre race requirement and without this you could not run. The race was the Barry 40 and was held on a running track in early March. This equates to just less than one hundred and sixty one laps of a four hundred metre track. Each competitor had to provide at least one lap counter for the event. Claire and her daughter Becky had volunteered to fulfil this role so I was good to go. Leading up to this race I went to our club track training sessions and just ran round the track for an hour. I was hoping that this would give me some of the mental strength that was required to cope with running round in circles. Some of my club mates suggested that I could end up with one leg shorter than the other if I completed this event. I went into the race believing they would probably get us to half way in one direction then turn us round to go in the other direction. Not so, we had to run the whole forty miles in an anti clockwise direction.

It was quite a low key event with less than thirty runners and only eighteen finished the race. I had set myself a target of completing each lap in less than two minutes which would give me a finish time of less than five hours. A table was placed at the side of the track where you put all your drinks and nourishment. You could stop as often as you liked for as long as you liked but the clock kept ticking. We set off at ten o'clock and almost immediately a group of about four runners broke away. I stuck to my pace estimate but found myself very near the back of the field. Claire and Becky held up posters with words of encouragement every few laps and this helped take my mind off the race. This worked well for me as I stuck to my pace and gradually started to go past people. After a couple of hours it started to become difficult to tell who was in front of whom because of all the stopping. The only thing Claire could tell me was that I was in the top half.

By the time we reached the marathon distance a few people had already dropped out. I was feeling pretty good and still banging out the laps in less than two minutes. I reached the thirty mile mark and was in the top ten and just a lap behind the first in my age group. Then I went through a really dodgy spell. I started to feel sick and my pace per lap dropped by ten or fifteen seconds. I honestly felt like packing it all in at that stage as I dropped down the field. I am not sure what kept me going but I battled through the next few miles and at about thirty five miles I started to feel good again. My pace increased to less than two minutes per lap again and I started to make up places. I can't tell you how difficult it is to go past the finish line a hundred and sixty times during a race. Every time you are struggling it seems so easy to just step off the track and call it a day, mentally that is so tough, but I kept going and by the end was making up ground on everyone.

After five hours and nine minutes of running round in circles I crossed the finish line, I was in sixth place and second in my age group. The winner completed in four hours and twenty eight minutes and the first in my age group was four and half minutes ahead of me, which was just over two laps.

Feeling happy with the result and how I had coped with this event, I felt I could get under the five hour mark, and vowed to come back the following year. I am not sure why but I never did and that was my only outing in a track ultra.

The next event on the calendar was the GL3D and Claire had decided she wanted to have a go this year as it was going 'On Tour' and was to take place in North Wales. This was like nothing she had ever done before and she was duly very nervous before the start. Day one saw us spending ten hours in the mountains. The coastal start was followed by a traverse of the Carnedd's before dropping down to the Ogwen valley and then back up and over the Glyders, with our finish near Capel Curig. The weather on the first day was glorious and we were crossing my favourite Snowdonia area, the Glyders. The rock formations along this ridge are just spectacular and the views over to Snowdon and back to the Carnedd's breathtaking. Unfortunately because it is so rocky it is a nightmare for running on. It is so difficult to get any sort of rhythm as you weave your way through the boulder fields and it just saps your strength. We were the last runners into camp but Claire was feeling very satisfied at having completed what was a long tough day in the mountains, plus she had seen areas of Snowdonia that she had never seen before.

On day two the weather returned to normal with heavy low cloud, strong winds and intermittent rain. Our route started with a climb up to the summit of Moel Siabod followed by a lovely two kilometre grassy descent heading in a westerly direction to Clogwyn Bwlch-y-Maen. From here we turned south along a very boggy ridge to Moel Druman. From this point we had to make our way to the summit of Snowdon via Yr Aran. This was without doubt the toughest section of the whole three days. After all the height gain we had to drop to a height of about fifty metres to cross the road before having to climb up to Yr Aran at seven hundred and seventy metres then straight down to Bwlch Cwm Llan, a descent of two hundred and fifty metres, then straight up the ridge to the summit of Snowdon at one thousand and eighty five metres. The approach to the summit of Snowdon was quite eerie, the mist was heavy and damp and as we got closer to the top there appeared, what looked like huge long necked creatures on the summit. This of course was the mechanical diggers that were up there as part of the cafe refurbishment, this meant the cafe was closed so no nice warming cup of tea for us. From the summit we were to head down the Pyg Track to Pen-y-Pass and then on down to Pen-y-Gwyrd

Hotel where a mini bus was waiting with a hot drink and a piece of cake, this was our day two finish and we were out for nine hours. Once again we were last and Claire was exhausted but also elated at having completed another gruelling day over this rugged terrain.

The final day had to get us back to the coast but to get there we were going to have to get over the Carnedd's once again. The weather was much the same as the previous day as we set off, but by the end it had cleared quite a bit to give us a fine end to the event. We spent another seven hours out which gave us a total of twenty six hours for the three days, and even though we were the last finishers, we finished, Claire was totally exhausted by the end and we had covered just about the whole of the Snowdon range.

Later that year I competed in the LAMM with Dave and the Saunders with Claire as well as numerous one day mountain events, so it was another year of off road and mountains.

In amongst all this off road running we had another target to achieve, and that was getting Claire a qualifying time for the 2008 London marathon which was three hours and forty five minutes. The first attempt was the Lochaber marathon where she missed out by just six seconds. Feeling bitterly disappointed we decided to try again at Edinburgh just five weeks later, and this time she qualified by over a minute. This meant we would both be running at London so serious training to be done in the early part of 2008.

It had been a good year and I was actually feeling the strongest I had felt since my best road running days. I am convinced that the switch to lots of off road running took the strain off my knees and had given me a way of gaining strength without pounding the pavements. I would still get times when I had to take a break because of my knees but after rest and a few Ibuprofen I was good to go. I had traditionally taken it easy in December because I was always looking to run a spring marathon which meant preparation would start in January. I always felt I trained better in those dark cold months mainly because my asthma did not affect me too much. The plan was to get London out of the way then head for the hills. The year started according to plan and the training was going really well until a skiing trip to the Pyrenees in mid February. I twisted my knee badly and over the next few months my running stuttered as I tried to recover. I eventually discovered I had a cartilage tear and would need some time out. Despite this I still went to London and tried to run, the race went appallingly as I set off with a three hour fifteen minute target in my head. The lack of training miles took its toll and my knee started to really hurt. I completed in three hours and twenty minutes but was in a lot of pain and decided to take time out from running.

The next few months were spent mostly on a bike, my knee eventually recovered but when I started running again I developed another injury. This time it was my foot, it felt like I had a stone bruise on my heel but after a visit to the doctor he told me I had Plantar Faciitus. I tried to do the LAMM with Dave in June but we had to drop out at the end of the first day because of my injury, however I did manage to complete the Saunders with Claire just a few weeks later, but after this I was out of running for another couple of months and I did not really get running again until September. I tried a couple of events in October but felt overweight and very sluggish and nearly dropped out of a couple of them.

The only other thing of note in 2008 was something that happened at Bitton Road Runners. While I was on holiday in the Lake District in June I had a call from one of the committee members, James Wade. He told me that our chairman at that time, Gordon Robbins, had resigned. I asked him what had happened and if Bob Sperring, our vice chairman, had stepped up to take on the role. He then told me that there had been an incident at the club and that Gordon and Bob had disagreed on who the guilty party was. There was a row and subsequently Gordon resigned as chairman and the following day Bob had resigned as vice chairman. This was all a bit of a shock because Gordon had been chairman at the club for many years and he definitely loved the role. The club had gone from strength to strength under his leadership and held one of the most popular off road races on the calendar, The Sodbury Slog, and Gordon was the race director. I was due back in Bristol at the weekend and I asked James to organise a committee meeting upon my return. He said he would do this but then told me he had spoken to other committee members and they had said that if the situation stayed as it was then they would like me to take the role of chairman. This was even more of a shock. I was very happy leading the coaching team but was not sure about sitting in the hot seat as chairman.

The committee meeting was held on my return and after some lengthy discussions I agreed that if all attempts to entice Gordon or Bob back on to the committee failed, then I would temporarily take on the role until the next AGM, which was in September.

I did my best to get to the bottom of what had happened but to be honest the only people who really know what took place on that evening were the two people involved. I spoke at length with both of them so I would get both sides of the story. I then organised a meeting between myself, Gordon and Bob to see if we could sort the issue and come to some amicable arrangement whereby they could both return to their positions on the committee. The situation was quite bad and already people were talking of supporting Gordon or supporting Bob. This was not good and there were rumours of people wanting to break away and form another club.

Once it was clear that neither of them was going to return I accepted the position of chairman, and set about making club nights as normal as possible, so people could get on with doing what they all wanted to do on club nights, go for a run. I will admit I struggled initially with all the politics going on behind the scenes but with the help of the committee we managed to steady the ship and get ourselves to the next AGM. During the four months leading up to the AGM I had spoken to as many people as I could within the club and felt I had a good understanding their issues and concerns. Myself and the committee came in for some very harsh criticism over these months but they all showed that if we stuck together and did what we felt was right then we could get through this. Some of the things that were said to me were biased and quite venomous. I will never repeat these things because I believe that some of them were said in the heat of the moment and, I would hope, they were later regretted.

I had told the committee that I did not want to stand for re-election, and was hoping that by the time the AGM came round there would a suitable club member ready to step forward and take on the role of chairman, so I could return to what I loved most, running and coaching. The division within the membership was still very apparent and as the date approached I was told that Gordon wanted to stand for chairman. I did not believe that this would be good for the club as it would reinforce the division that already existed, so I decided that if no other club member came forward then I would stand again. Just before the AGM Gordon decided that instead of chairman he would just run for election to the committee. This was only going to be a good thing for the committee, his years of experience would help us and it meant he was still in a position to carry out the role of the Sodbury Slog race director.

I was a bag of nerves on the night of the AGM but did my best to sound relaxed and confident. I was re-elected as chairman and Gordon was on the committee. The rest of the committee was re-elected and for the first time I felt as though we could move forward as a club and put aside the issues of the previous months. The ginger haired, freckled character with the stammer had certainly come a long way. He was now chairman and lead coach of a three hundred strong running club.

Moving forward as a unified club was easier said than done and it took a long time for the club to really settle down again. Having said this it had settled enough by the time of the next AGM the following year, for me to step down as chairman and return to coaching. It also meant I started to focus on ultra marathons again and three of these events had caught my eye. They were different in their concept and their challenge but I felt I was ready to start preparing for them, as long as I could stay injury free.

23 A DAY IN THE LAKES

"How to run an ultramarathon ? Puff out your chest, put one foot in front of the other, and don't stop till you cross the finish line."
— Dean Karnazes

The first of these three ultra events had been on my radar for a couple of years and on Bryan's. We had both done a few recces and Bryan had even had a couple of aborted attempts, the earliest of these was in 2008. The event was the Joss Naylor Lakeland Challenge or the old man's Bob Graham as it was affectionately known. With Steve Jones as my marathon hero and Bruce Fordyce as my ultra marathon hero, Joss Naylor was without doubt my mountain running hero. He was a phenomenal mountain runner and if mountain running had been an Olympic sport then he would have been an Olympic champion.

When Bryan and myself started to look at this event we were both in the 50-54 age group, and the target time was set at sub twelve hours. After doing a few sections of the course I decided that twelve hours was a bit too fast for me, so I continued to do sections of it with a view to having a go once I was in the 55-59 age group, when I would have fifteen hours to complete the course. The route starts at Pooley Bridge and goes on to traverse 30 summits covering a distance of 48 miles with 5182 metres of ascent and finishing on Greendale Bridge close to the home of the great man himself. When Joss completed this route he was fifty four years old and in very bad weather with heavy rain and a strong SW wind he completed the run to Greendale Bridge in 11 hours and 30 minutes.

I knew I would need perfect conditions to stand any chance of completing this route within fifteen hours and had decided that on one of our holidays in the Lake District I would just pick the day at the last minute. This would mean my attempt would be unofficial but as long as I completed it then I would be happy. My first attempt was in July 2010 and from very early on I knew it was going to end in failure. I set off in good conditions from Pooley Bridge, but the weather rapidly deteriorated and between Kirkstone Pass and Dunmail Raise it poured with rain, so I aborted. It had taken me six hours in awful conditions to get to Dunmail and I knew that the first half was easier than the second, but I took a lot of confidence from this attempt as I had now completed both halves on separate occasions in a reasonable time. I did not get another opportunity to have a go until the following year when we were again on holiday in the Lake District.

In early June of that year I completed the LAMM with Dave and on the second and third of July I completed the Saunders with Claire. Both events had gone well and I felt I was in good condition. After the Saunders myself and Claire were due to holiday in the Lakes for two weeks. We spent the first week walking and mountain biking and then I saw that the weather forecast for the following Wednesday was very good. As the weather in mountain areas is very unpredictable I told Claire that I might try the Joss on Wednesday 13th July. I did not make a final decision until the Tuesday when the forecast confirmed that Wednesday was due to be a misty and damp start to the day but then this would clear to leave a dry warm sunny day.

I relaxed as much as possible on Monday and Tuesday and set myself for a 5am start on Wednesday. We were staying in Thornthwaite so the drive to the start was only thirty minutes. It was certainly a cool and misty start to the day and by the time we got to Pooley Bridge I was a bag of nerves. I stood on the bridge just before my start time as Claire took some photo's. At exactly 5am I set off from Pooley Bridge. I had done this start a couple of times and usually ran along the road and around to the campsite before heading up to the ridge and the first checkpoint Arthur's Pike, but because I had seen a footpath along the river that then cut across the fields to the campsite I decided to go that way. This was a mistake, when the footpath petered out I found myself in unfamiliar fields and could not find a way out. I had to back track to get back up to the road and along to the campsite. The way through the back of the campsite and on to the hills is not that clear but I had done this a few times and stuck with what I knew. By the time I reached Arthur's Pike I was already five minutes down on my schedule, not the best start to a long day. The ridge from this point on up to High Street is not too steep and mostly good running on soft turf, if at times too soft, but pretty good underfoot. When I reached High Street I had made up a couple of minutes of that lost time. The mist was starting to clear and I was beginning to settle down and enjoy the challenge. This part of the route is definitely the easiest and it is not until you start the descent from Thornthwaite Beacon to Stoney Cove Pike that you get to more rocky and technical terrain. From Stoney Cove Pike it's a straightforward run down to the first road crossing at Kirkstone Pass. When I arrived I was only a minute behind schedule but feeling good and positive. It was still only eight thirty so it was still cool but the mist had all but cleared and it looked like I was in for a clear and sunny day. Claire met me at Kirkstone with what was going to be my nourishment both here, and at the only other road crossing at Dunmail, a cup of tea and a jam sandwich. After a five minute stop I was on my way and climbing Red Screes. From the summit of Red Screes there is a nice, if a bit boggy, run across to Hart Crag then along the head of the Fairfield Horseshoe to the summit of Fairfield. The descent from Fairfield and the climb up Seat Sandal is another rocky and technical section and really gives you an indication of what is yet to come. From the summit of Seat Sandal I headed off in a north westerly direction to pick up the path along Raise Beck that would take me down to Dunmail. I was now back on schedule and Claire was there to welcome me with a hot drink and a jam sandwich. This would be the last I would see of her until near the finish. She was going to park at Greendale and then run towards me, hopefully meeting me near Pillar, and then she would run with me to the finish. From Dunmail comes the first real big test of the day, the climb up Steel Fell. This climb is both steep and relentless and as I had already been out for six hours I was not looking forward to this. The sun was up and the temperature was steadily rising as I slogged my way three hundred metres up the face of Steel Fell.

I finally reached the summit after nearly thirty minutes of climbing and when I looked around me the whole of the Lake District lay before me. To the north lay Thirlmere Lake, the Helvellyn Range and Skiddaw in the distance. To the south lay Helm Crag, Grasmere and Lake Windermere. To the east I was looking back at the ground I had covered including Seat Sandal and Fairfield. To the west the long ridge to High Raise, and in the distance, Bowfell, Esk Pike, Great End, Great Gable and Pillar. This westerly view was a sharp reminder of what I still had to do to complete this challenge. I was feeling pretty good but I also knew the real tough stuff was yet to come.

From Steel Fell there is a long boggy ridge run before a fairly steep climb on to the High Raise plateau and then a kilometre run across to the trig point on the summit. This is nearly an hour of running followed by another fifty minutes to get from here to Rossett Pike. These two sections are particularly tough because of the terrain and the distance between the summits. Once on Rossett Pike I was then faced with the ascent of Bowfell. There is a sort of a track that runs from the south side of Angle Tarn and cuts diagonally across the face of Bowfell and brings you out not far from the summit. It looks very steep and rocky but once you are on the track it weaves its way through and you are on the summit in thirty minutes. Once here I knew that this was the highest point of the day and that I was on the final ridge. This is no reason to relax because the route from here becomes very rocky, very tricky and very technical, right up until the summit of Haycock.

There are three really difficult descents along this section and at the first one I had a tough decision to make. From the summit of Great End I had to decide whether to continue north and pick my way down through The Band to Sty Head or, as I chose, turn round and run back the way I had come and turn north at the earliest opportunity dropping down to pick up the track that runs past Sprinkling Tarn and then to Sty Head. I had tried on several occasions to find my way through The Band to Sty Head but had failed every time, hence the decision to back track. It just felt wrong turning round to go back the way I had come, but it was definitely the right decision for me as I made it to Sty Head in less than twenty five minutes.

Standing at the Sty Head stretcher box I looked up at my next summit, Great Gable, it was some 470 metres higher than where I was standing and it was very steep. I was now about thirty minutes ahead of schedule and convinced myself that even if I struggled to get to this top I would still have time in hand. I set off, and to my own amazement, I reached the summit cairn to find I had gained another five minutes.

The descent from Great Gable is the next tricky one, and as I had done on all my trial runs I went too far left and ended up in the loose scree. I gingerly made my way down and thankfully had only lost a couple of minutes. Next up was Kirkfell, another steep climb but less than 200 metres of height gain on this one. Once on the summit it's nearly a kilometre across to the summit cairn and the descent is one of the trickiest on this ridge.

I arrived at Black Sail Pass to find I had gained another few minutes. I was desperately tired and low on water and food but my spirits were lifted by the knowledge that Claire was heading towards me with both of these, and to be perfectly honest after eleven hours of solo running I was desperate for some company.

It is a long slow ascent from Black Sail Pass up to Pillar, I had allowed an hour on my schedule, but I just put my head down and slogged my way up. My legs were now screaming at me to stop and rest but in my usual style my head was down and I was just putting one foot in front of the other. No climb goes on forever, I just needed to keep going and the summit would come to me. Three quarters of the way up and I heard a most welcome voice, it was Claire, and I don't think I have ever been so happy to see someone. I took on some water and food and after checking my watch I found I was nearly forty minutes up on my fifteen hour schedule. It was now just a case of keeping going and making sure I did not do anything stupid.

After a couple of minutes we set off and I think Claire thought we were in a 5k race. She set off so quick that within a couple of minutes she was about fifty metres ahead of me. I called out to her and explained that she had to move at my pace, she did not need to drag me along because I had plenty of time in hand. From Pillar it is a short descent to Wind Gap followed by an even shorter ascent to Scoat Fell. Then there is the out and back section to get to the summit of Steeple. It is only ten minutes out and back but quite a tricky little section. The next summit is Haycock, once again very straightforward and once I had reached this point I was able look down upon my two remaining summits, Seatallan and Middle Fell. They were below me, how difficult could they be? Well let me tell you the ascent of Seatallan was purgatory. My legs had gone completely as I trudged my way up this steep but fairly short climb and I needed all of Claire's words of encouragement to get me there. Once there I knew everything was going to be fine. I had time in hand and only one more summit to make. Seatallan to Middle Fell took thirty minutes and from there it was downhill all the way.

We started the descent and after ten minutes Greendale came in to view down in the valley. I could see the car parked at the bottom and my only thought was to get down, put my feet up and let Claire feed me while plying me with copious amounts of hot tea. This last descent is just a winding grassy track and was not going to cause me any problems I thought, until Claire went over on her ankle and fell into the ferns. I stopped to see how she was but she could not stand. I looked at my watch then at the car below and could not believe I was so close. I eventually helped Claire to her feet and she managed to start hobbling. She told me to continue on down and finish and she would make her way slowly down. I took the car keys from her and ran down to Greendale. I reached the bridge in a time of fourteen hours and twenty minutes, but I did not have time to celebrate. I ran over to the car and looked back up the hillside where Claire was making her way slowly down to the car. Thank goodness she was going to make it under her own steam because I am not sure if I would have been able to get back up the hill to help her.

She finally made it to the car but her ankle was very painful and swollen so she had to sit down and take the weight off it immediately. It was clear that she would not be able to drive or even do much else, so after fourteen hours in the mountains I had to sit Claire down and make her tea as well as feed her before driving us back to Thornthwaite to a warm comfortable bed. I told Claire to ring Bryan and tell him what I had done. He did not even know I was going to make an attempt and he congratulated me. I also told him my time so he now had a target for when he made his attempt. It was on this drive back to Thornthwaite that the fact that I had completed this route began to sink in. I had been thinking about this for years and I had done it on my own with the minimum of support. It was a very contented, if very tired runner, who slept so well that night.

24   5-DUNMAIL TO LANGDALE

"I don't run to add days to my life, I run to add life to my days."
– Ronald Rook

To start leg six I crossed the main road and started the run along the western side of Thirlmere. After a kilometre or so of road there was a left turn and then the start of the climb by Dob Gill up to Harrop Tarn. From the first part of the climb it was very wet and muddy. I knew when we reached the main ridge and made our way towards High Tove that this would only get worse. This ridge is the southernmost part of the Ullscarf Ridge. It is without doubt the wettest, muddiest part of the Lake District. I had the unfortunate pleasure of having to run the whole of this ridge during a mountain marathon a few years earlier and it was five miles of torture. The bogs are so bad that it's almost impossible to get any sort of running going. Luckily we would only be doing a mile or so of this ridge and this positive thought kept me going during a very tough climb.

I had underestimated how much of a climb this was and even after passing Harrop Tarn it was still a long way to Blea Tarn. At this point I was on my own and I was finding it quite difficult to run as much as I should have. The thing with Ultra Marathons is you find yourself on your own a lot so the mental strength required to keep moving is immense. I was on my own through the woods up to Harrop Tarn and beyond but as I made the main ridge by Blea Tarn I saw a few runners in front of me. As we made our way across the bog, which turned out to be as muddy as I expected, I was just thankful I was doing this section in daylight. The race instructions had said that if you reached the end of leg six in the dark then, in the interests of safety, you would have to wait until 19.00pm for a group guided run to Watendlath.

I started to make up ground on a couple of people in front of me, but once again was struggling to get into any sort of running rhythm, even though I was feeling quite strong. The pain in my knee had subsided and most of the negative thoughts had disappeared during this tough and demanding section. The flag markers led us up to High Tove and then in a straight line down to Watendlath.

I spent about ten minutes here and spoke with other runners as well as the people manning the feed station. I took on lots of fluids but decided to forego the Sticky Toffee pudding. I felt I needed to get going, and get going quickly, as this was the longest section of the event at nine and a half miles, and I would need every ounce of energy and determination if I was to reach Langdale before dark.

I was familiar with the decent into the Borrowdale valley, having walked, run and cycled this particular section. I also knew it was a long way along the Langstrath valley before the steep ascent of Stake Pass.

I made good time on the descent from Watendlath and soon reached the valley floor at Rosthwaite. It was then a couple of kilometres along the Cumbria Way, a well defined if rocky track, before turning right into Langstrath. Once in Langstrath we crossed over the footbridge to the right hand side of the valley, the Cumbria Way continued on the left hand side. I have run both sides of this valley and no matter which side you are on the other side always looks easier. The truth of the matter is they are as difficult as each other.

The valley floor is reasonably flat but the path is very rocky. I managed to run most of it without burning myself out. I was trying to save as much energy as possible for the ascent of Stake Pass. We picked up the Cumbria Way again as we started the ascent and I was determined get over this obstacle as quickly as possible. I passed a few people on this ascent and reached the top with renewed confidence, determined to get to Stickle Barn Tavern before dark. The Cumbria Way would take us all the way down into the Mickleden valley and on to Langdale, but it was a long way, even when we reached the valley floor it was nearly five kilometres of rocky paths. Once again I was in familiar territory and in a place I loved, with the Langdale fells surrounding me.

The light was starting to fade as I made the valley floor and with that the temperature was starting to drop. I forced myself on even though at one point I thought I had missed the turning for the tavern. It just seemed to go on and on as the light faded more and more.

As I made my way toward the tavern I spotted another runner ahead of me. This spurred me on and I tried to catch him before Stickle Barn. Finally there was the marker to turn off the track and into the tavern, I was just a few metres behind the other runner but was so relieved to reach this point while we still had a little bit of light.

I stumbled into the Tavern only to be greeted by a Race Marshall who said "well done but I'm afraid you have missed the cut off time by ten minutes, take a seat and get some refreshments and we will arrange transport to get you to the finish". I was absolutely dumbstruck, "are you sure?" I asked him. "yes" he replied "7.30 pm was the cut off and you have just missed it". I could not believe what I was hearing all that effort up to this point had counted for nothing. I walked into the Tavern to find plenty of other runners tucking into chips, sandwiches and plenty of drinks. I looked at the faces around me and could tell who was still in the race. They had full kit on and were also putting on head torches. I could also tell the ones who were out of the race, they sat dejected and forlorn, some even looked relieved as they knew their race was over.

I sat down feeling absolutely shattered and hugely disappointed, I was struggling to comprehend how I had missed the cut off time when I thought I was going so well. My body ached and my knee started to hurt again. Ten minutes later I was still struggling to take it all in but for me it was all over and I was out of the race.

BILL GRAHAM

Distance covered 50.8 miles
Time taken 13hrs 17mins 53secs
Overall position at Watendlath 45th
Overall position at Dunmail 41st

25 A GREEN MAN

"Even when you have gone as far as you can, and everything hurts, and you are staring at the spectre of self-doubt, you can find a bit more strength deep inside you, if you look closely enough."
— *Hal Higdon*

Buoyed by the Joss Naylor success we returned to Bristol and I was looking forward to some positive running on the back of such a great run. Unfortunately I suffered for weeks afterwards and my running was not good. In fact I spent more time cycling than running throughout that summer. It was October before I really got back into my old running routine and even then I seemed to be struggling for speed. I was finding that the normal road races I had been doing for years no longer interested me and was finding it difficult to motivate myself to run on the road. I did not race again at all in 2011 but towards the end of the year I did start some quality sessions on the track.

In the early part of 2011 a friend at work had mentioned a challenge that I might be interested in. This challenge involved circumnavigating Bristol by following the Community Forest Path around the city. The distance was forty five miles and anyone who completed this challenge had their name entered into the Forestal Book of the Honourable Order of Woodwoses. This book was held by the Gaveller whose name was Chris Bloor. I went online and had a look at the details and became interested. There were route descriptions online so I printed them off and decided to try a few sections and see how I got on. Chris had divided the course into eight legs and in my first run I did legs four to seven. Within this leg you have to run through a housing estate called Bradley Stoke, and this is where I got totally lost.

Through the rest of 2011 I tried a few other legs with mixed success and was beginning to think I would never be able to put all this together in one continuous run. Then towards the end of the year the Utrarunning website was advertising it as a new race for March 2012. How could I resist, an ultra race that was on my doorstep and I could do practice runs on it every day of the week if I wanted to. In fact I would have to run the route as much as possible if I wanted to find my way round without getting lost.

I immediately entered the race and this gave me the drive and enthusiasm to get out on the course as much as I could. The course itself is on and off road with a few hills and lots of mud. For the race you had to self navigate so I was determined to know the course back to front before March, and the back to front part would come in handy a couple of years later. Throughout January and February I ran the course as much as I could and ironed out all the tricky sections, so by race day I had no worries about which way to go.

Race day arrived and the weather was dry, warm and sunny. There had been plenty of rain leading up to the event so the course was still very muddy but conditions were about as good as you could expect in early March. Thirty seven people were on the start line and thirty three finished. Bryan was on the start line with me and we were running together towards our first checkpoint when he had to answer the call of nature. I continued expecting to see him a little later but did not see him again until the end.

After the first checkpoint I found myself running on my own for a bit but then picked up another competitor just before checkpoint two and he decided to stay with me once I had told him I knew the course and there was no way we were going to get lost. At that time we were running well and I was maintaining the pace I wanted. We reached the checkpoint just after half way and from there I really struggled for a few miles over what was an easy part of the course. Even though I felt I was struggling my time over each legs told me I was still achieving the pace I wanted. The other competitor was still with me and before we finished we managed to overtake one or two people. Over the last couple of miles I started to struggle again and Claire ran out to meet me on the Clifton Suspension Bridge before willing me along to the finish line at Redwood Lodge. I had been out for eight hours and this placed me fourth overall and first veteran. The nice thing about the race was having the support of fellow club runners on the route, as the course passed very close to Bitton on its journey round Bristol. I even stopped at Warmley station for a doughnut and some coffee while chatting to some club members. I was exhausted at the end but I had made it to the finish line before it got dark and done it in just under eight hours, or so I thought.

My official time for the race was eight hours and one minute. My stopwatch and Claire's both said seven hours fifty nine minutes and twenty five seconds. When I questioned my time I was told that it was definitely eight hours and one minute. I was just about ready to accept this when I realised that the time keeper was using the time on his phone to allocate race times. So he was assuming that we had started at exactly eight o'clock that morning and as I had finished at one minute past four on his phone then that was our time. If you look at the times for that year and the next two years they are all rounded to the nearest minute. It was not until 2015 that runner's times had hours minutes and seconds.

Now you may think I am complaining about nothing important but I was desperate to get under eight hours and I believe I did. Imagine if as a marathon runner you had never run under four hours and then in a particular race you ran three hours fifty nine minutes and fifty nine seconds. You would be overjoyed until an official told you they rounded it to the nearest minute so your time was four hours. I did have this conversation with Steve Worrallo the race organiser, and I understand that I will have to live with eight hours one minute as my official time but it will always be under eight hours for me. The other thing I will point out is that the first few races were nearly two miles longer because the start was at the Redwood Lodge Hotel which is about a mile away from the original Green Man route. So the times gained in those events are probably worth ten to fifteen minutes less than published.

From this very modest start the race has gone from strength to strength and now accepts around two hundred and fifty runners. The course has changed a little bit over the years due to the requests of a couple of land owners and a golf course. As the numbers grew they were worried about the damage two hundred plus runners could make in some areas of the off road sections so the route was diverted around these.

Two years after the original event the organisers came up with the Midnight Express idea. This was to be held in August over the Green Man route but done in reverse and at starting at 11pm. If the Green Man had a modest start then the Midnight Express start was even more so. Just ten runners started and only eight finished that first event. I ran and completed in eight and a half hours, this put me in second place and first veteran. The event only ran for three years and never really generated great interest, the highest number of runners was thirty.

After I had completed this event I started to look around at other ultra races trying to find a different challenge. There seemed to be a lot to choose from as the hunger for a different kind of challenge took hold of the running community. A few people from Bitton Road Runners had expressed an interest in longer distances and one of those, Ira Rainey, approached me about the Green Man. I had known Ira for a few years and had mentored him when he approached me about his marathon aspirations. Ira's account of his journey to competing in the Green Man is all very well documented in his book Fat Man to Green Man, so I will not go into detail here. I would recommend this book to anyone who has any aspirations towards running an ultra marathon.

I always ran this race as eight legs as per the original Chris Bloor format. The race itself had different legs and checkpoints but I always used these eight legs to divide the course into fairly even times. Of those original eight legs my target was complete each leg in about an hour. Some were a little quicker and some a little slower but these times I allocated always let me know how I was doing. I ran the event on five occasions and completed it on three occasions. I dropped out twice. One of the completions was when I ran with Claire in her first attempt which she did in nine and a half hours. The first time I dropped out was because I was injured going into the race, but thought I would just do it and see how far I got. The second time I dropped out was in 2017 after feeling totally exhausted before we even got to the halfway point. This turned out to be the start of something that took nearly two years to sort out and initially made me think that I had reached an age when these running events were beyond me, but more of that later.

Over the next few years I was running mainly with the view of doing ultra races. I even entered a few but never made the start line because of various issues with fitness and the logistics of some of these events. I found I was running less and biking more. Claire and myself had road and mountain bikes and seemed to be spending more and more time on them. Bryan had suffered a recurring calf muscle injury and was also doing more on the bike.

He discovered the Chain Reaction series of events which seemed to dominate what we did for a couple of years. The format was to arrive at a location on Friday evening. Do fifty miles or a hundred miles on the road on Saturday. Sunday was the main event which was a choice of about four distances ranging from twenty five kilometres to eighty kilometres off road. The locations were places like Crickhowell in South Wales, Ruthin in North Wales, Llandovery in South Wales and Kilnsey in the Yorkshire Dales. It was quite a sight seeing two hundred or so mountain bike riders heading through small villages on their way to a day out in the hills. These epic events entailed two days of tough riding which took up the weekend. We were also using the bikes while on holiday whenever we could.

All this meant I was doing less running but strangely enough, when I did run it was over long distances. I even had a go at a few legs of the Bob Graham round to see how I coped. I came to the conclusion that at the age I was and the speed I was capable of at that time meant the Bob Graham was probably a step too far. The Bob Graham Round is 42 peaks across the Lake District and is one of the most demanding challenges in England, with approximately 28,500ft of ascent over a distance of 74 miles. It starts at the Moot Hall in Keswick and you have twenty four hours to complete the round. You also need a good backup team plus people to run with you on each section. In 2018 Kilian Jornet beat the record set by Billy Bland in 1982. He knocked an hour off Billy's time to set the new record of 12hrs and 52mins. After having completed a few legs of this challenge you can only sit back and be amazed at this achievement. I am not sure I would be able to do it but I would love to have a go. Maybe one day I will, who knows.

At this time I felt I was drifting along with no purpose and running less and less, so to try and drag myself out of the doldrums I put in an entry for the Green Man which was in March 2017. The preparation did not go at all well as I struggled to get the miles in, I just felt tired all the time, and on the day I dropped out. I started well enough but after a couple of hours I felt the energy just drain away from me. I was really disappointed and could not understand why a few years ago I was contemplating more ultra marathons while currently I was struggling to run for more than an hour. It was on a routine visit to the doctor later that year that I had my first inclination that all was not right with me, and a few months later I began to understand why I had been feeling the way I did.

26 TOO TIRED TO RUN

"What I've learned from running is that the time to push hard is when you're hurting like crazy and you want to give up. Success is often just around the corner."
—James Dyson

2017 was not a great year for me, at the beginning of the year I was finding it really difficult to get any sort of routine into my training and my energy levels were the lowest they had ever been. Was this just an age issue, and was my time of running long distances now over. I battled on trying to do what I could and then in August, following my annual health check with my GP, I received a phone call from the surgery asking me to come back and do another blood test. They had seen what they described as an anomaly. My ferritin level was unusually high so they wanted to take another test just to verify that it was a one off. When the results of the second test were reviewed I was called in to see the doctor. The second test had also shown a very high level of ferritin in my blood. Ferritin is a protein that stores iron, releasing it when your body needs it. The normal male adult level is measured as ng/ml and is between 20 and 250. Mine had come back with a reading of over one thousand. The doctor explained that I could have a condition called Haemochromatosis. The symptoms associated with this condition are, fatigue, weakness, joint pain (particularly the fingers), erectile dysfunction, chest pain and shortness of breath. As I was suffering from all of these and the condition was genetic the doctor said he was going to refer me to the Bristol Royal Infirmary so they could check if I carried the gene. He said that the BRI would decide on the course of treatment. It was two months before I had the test at the BRI and a couple of weeks later they called to tell me that I carried the gene and that they were going to refer me to the Haematology Department to start treatment. It was another three months before my appointment and by the time I attended my ferritin level was one thousand eight hundred and fifty.

Before I attended the haematology appointment I also discovered I had eczema. I had been suffering with a bit of rash for a good twelve months or so and in September of that year my skin was on fire the whole time. I was finding it really uncomfortable to run off road as any contact with long grass made my legs itch so bad I had to stop. It felt like someone was jabbing me with pins all over my body and the continuous scratching was making my skin bleed. To combat this condition I was put on a course of tablets that would lower my immune system. It was a few weeks before they had any effect and I had to continue on these tablets for eighteen months before I was able to come off them without the rash flaring up again.

Then in October I had an accident while playing five a side football. I realise that maybe I was bit too old to be playing football but I had been playing once week for about three months and was really enjoying it. Then in one game I took an awkward fall and ruptured my patella tendon. In the fall I had hyper extended the knee which caused the kneecap to tear away from the tendon. As I fell I knew it was bad and this was confirmed by the player nearest me who took one look at my knee and had to walk away. Basically my kneecap was now about two inches higher than it should have been. My quads had retracted and as my kneecap was no longer attached to my tendon the kneecap was pulled upwards. The accident happened at a sports centre just a few hundred metres from the A&E department of Southmead Hospital. I was loaded in to a car and driven over to the hospital where I waited about three hours to be seen. I was desperately trying to hold my kneecap in the right position whilst I was waiting, convinced that I had dislocated it and that they would just pop it back into place for me. When I was eventually seen I was told that it was a rupture and I would need surgery as soon as possible. They strapped my knee and sent me home on crutches and asked me to return in the morning. As a coincidence I was due to come into the hospital the following morning to see the dermatologist about my eczema. Claire drove me to the hospital at 8.30 in the morning where I attended my dermatology appointment before hobbling across to wait in another department. They promised they would try to do the surgery that day but could not make any promises. I just had to sit and wait and was allowed only sips of water to see me through the day. At one point the nurse saw me fidgeting and squirming in my seat and asked me if I would like to move to another more comfortable seat. It was not the seat that was bothering me it was where I was seated. I was in a main corridor and throughout the morning people were walking past me with cups of tea and coffee and were carrying cakes, biscuits and savouries. I was not allowed any of this in case I ended up in theatre and it was driving me mad. I asked if she could move me to an area where I would not be able to see all this food and drink going past me, so in the afternoon I was sat in a quiet little corridor on my own.

After a few hours of waiting I was beginning to give up hope and was in a lot of pain and discomfort. Then the nurse approached me and told me I would be going down for surgery between 4.30 and 5.30 and as long as I could eat, drink and pee following the operation then I could go home that evening. I was eventually taken to theatre at around 5pm, and as is the case with general anaesthetic, I awoke two hours later in the recovery room not sure where I was or what had happened and with my leg in a brace. The nurse was speaking to me and told me everything had gone well and would I like a drink and something to eat. Tea and toast came immediately to mind, I had not eaten or drank since 10pm the previous day. After drinking four cups of tea and three pieces of toast I felt ready for the trip to the toilet. They gave me a pair of crutches and asked me to make my own way to the loo, which was at the end of the room. I was a bit nervous but managed to make my own way there. The brace on my knee kept my leg straight and I quickly got the hang of walking on the crutches. They now decided I was ok to go home and started to sort out some pain killers for me to take home with me. I had been on liquid morphine while in hospital and they gave me some tablets to take when I was home. As I was already dosed up with pain killers they told me not take the tablets until about two in the morning.

Claire picked me up and by the time we got home it was about nine. I went straight to bed as I was feeling drowsy and immediately fell asleep. At about midnight I was woken by the feeling of someone sticking a screwdriver in my knee and wiggling it about. The morphine had worn off. For the next two hours I was in the worst pain I had ever felt. My knee felt like it was going to explode and I lay in bed in complete agony. The pain was excruciating and the next couple of hours were the longest two hours of my life. I spent the next few days counting down the clock to my next dose of pain killers. I have never known pain like it and hope to never experience it again. At my follow on appointment a week later I told the surgeon about the pain and he was not surprised because the surgery involved them making a six inch cut down over the joint. Then they drilled through the kneecap and fed sutures through the kneecap to attach it to the tendon, these were then pulled tight until the tendon and the kneecap were touching. Then when they were finished they bent the knee as far as they could to make sure the sutures would hold. My brace was replaced by a new one that would allow them to increase the range of movement angle each week and this was on my knee for eight weeks. I went through physiotherapy sessions for a few months to increase the range of movement and to restore the muscles that had deteriorated so much over those couple of months. It was three months before I could walk unaided, a further month before I could pedal through a full stroke on a bike and eight months before I ran again, and this run was just three laps of a football pitch in a local park. It was a long time before I felt strong enough to get out running for a few miles and even longer before I risked my knee in a true off road environment.

The treatment for haemochromatosis was so much simpler than this. You lie back in a chair and a needle is used to drain a small amount of blood, usually about 500ml, from a vein in your arm. This is done on a weekly basis until you are down to an acceptable level. My level was so high it took eight months of weekly bloodletting to get the level below a hundred. If you consider that Blood Donors give blood about once every twelve weeks, as this is considered the acceptable amount of time between donations, then I was a bit worried about giving every week. Throughout the eight month period I only had to miss two sessions due to low haemoglobin levels, so I seemed to cope quite well with the routine. The real problem with a weekly session was that it left me feeling washed out for a couple of days, so any training had to be done in the other five days, and even then I was not at my best as I was still recovering from my knee surgery.

After about five months, my ferritin levels were down to near the maximum acceptable level of 250 and my energy levels just started to go up. My knee was getting better and the muscles stronger so I was training harder, running for longer and my whole body was feeling energised. The target the haematology department had set for me was to get below the fifty mark and as I reached the lower levels the weekly decrease became smaller and smaller. When it finally reached a level of less than fifty they then said I could come back every three months and that should be enough to keep me at an acceptable level.

The one thing that I was concerned about during this treatment was that all the blood they were taking from me was going into the bin. The ferritn levels were too high for the blood to be of any use for blood donations. So now the levels were lower and they wanted me to come back every three months, I asked if I could get my ongoing treatment by donating blood quarterly. At first they were unsure but eventually I was accepted and now keep my ferritin at an acceptable level by donating blood every three months. It is nice to know that my blood is going in to the system to help those in need.

So finally my ferritin levels were under control, my eczema was under control and my knee was starting to feel stronger. I did not have full range of movement in that knee but I had enough to do what I wanted to do, which was cycle and run. Slowly I started to build up my strength and stamina and gradually increased the cycling and running distances, but would I be able to compete over the distances I used to compete at, only time would tell.

27 A WORLD OF RUNNING

"I run because long after my footprints fade away, maybe I will have inspired a few to reject the easy path, hit the trails, put one foot in front of the other, and come to the same conclusion I did: I run because it always takes me where I want to go."
– Dean Karnazes

I have been running since I can remember, I have been running competitively since I used to race against my brother when we were children. I am fiercely competitive and I love the feeling you get when you know you are running at your best. I have no shame in saying that I want people to admire what I have achieved, who wouldn't. But in the end all that matters is how you feel about your running. I have had more than my fair share of ups and downs but even now I still get a real buzz from running. I have progressed from pounding the pavements to running in some amazing locations off road. This still excites me and I can only think myself blessed to have been able to continue running, with only a couple of lay-offs, for nearly forty years.

I never dreamt at the start of my marathon ambitions in 1981 that I would still be running beyond the age of sixty. I have made every mistake in the book over the years and hopefully I have been able to pass on to people newer to this sport some of the knowledge I have gained. I still see people making the same mistakes as I did and have always tried to guide others. Some are keen to listen and learn while others continue doing the same things in the same way and wonder why they do not progress.

Every runner has a story to tell and most fellow runners like to hear those stories. Some of the comments I have heard over the years from fellow athletes have made me despair, sad, and laugh out loud. When I asked one particular athlete why he had given up track sessions after only taking part in a couple he replied "the sessions are ok but I can't get on with all that stopping and starting, why don't we just run 5k straight off?".

Another athlete when asked why he went off so quickly in marathon races but always died in the last six replied "I need to be at least 5 or 10 minutes up by halfway because I die in the last six".

Or the athlete who asked a coach "why if I do all my training, including long runs, at 9 minute miles can I not go any quicker in races?".

And finally standing at the start line of the Bitton 5k, which, as explained by the organiser, was a straight out and back course, one athlete piped up "how far is it to the turn round point?".

Don't you just love them, there are definitely some queer characters in running, in fact, most of us are a bit odd. Who else would get up at six in the morning in the middle of winter to punish themselves in a three hour run just for fun.

So what is this running thing all about? Why do we drive ourselves through the pain and discomfort of it all? What do we gain from the whole experience? I think we all get something different but I believe the recognition for our efforts from fellow athletes and people we know is a very important part of the process. As I have already said, my early years were quite driven by a need to be accepted by others and my sporting prowess was a way of gaining that acceptance. You do not have to be out there winning races you just need to be out there taking part. The competition we gain from racing with athletes of our own level is the main driving force to continuous improvement.

When I returned from South Africa in 1985 I initially found it difficult to regain the momentum in my running. It was only when I joined a club and trained with others that the competitive force returned. I had achieved a seventy five minute half marathon time in South Africa but was only just getting below eighty minutes upon my return to the UK. Once I had started training with a club I began to run more races and over a few half marathons my time had started to improve slightly. I was now getting around seventy eight minutes. I had also noticed a small group of runners from another club who always seemed to run together and always finished a couple of minutes ahead of me. So I decided that if I saw this group at the next half marathon race I was going to run with them. This happened at the Weston Half in September 1986 and as the race started I latched on to the back of the five man group. The early stages were comfortable enough and I sat at the back of the group and occasionally tried to make conversation with the five. They did not seem that interested and I overheard one of them remark "Don't worry I have seen him at a few races and we'll drop him before we get to ten". I felt this a bit rude and unsporting. If I was in their position I would have been encouraging me to hang in there and stay with the group. This one little comment made me even more determined than before, so I just sat at the back of the group and said nothing. Over the next couple of miles they put in a couple of slightly quicker bursts but still I hung on. When we got to about ten miles I was actually feeling quite good, but I did not push on at that point, I waited until eleven miles then put in a real effort for about a mile. This effort broke them and I ran away from the group and finished in the quickest time I had recorded since my return from South Africa. Three weeks later I achieved a marathon personal best and I never looked at that group again. I had beaten them and felt that from now on they would always be behind me. That is how continuous improvement works. Once you have beaten that target you have had for some time, never look back, look ahead at the next target.

While I had been running without that competitive experience I was treading water. It was only when that competition returned that I really started to thrive again and became focussed on targets. I would regularly set myself targets and worked really hard to attain those goals. Now I still enjoy my running and find it more satisfying than ever. I just love that hour or so of time to mull things over. It is quite amazing how running can bring clarity to things that can seem confused and muddled in your day to day life.

When you put yourself on the start line of a race you are making a massive commitment because you are the only one who can see this through. Nobody else can run for you, nobody else can make the decisions you make during the event and nobody else can drive you to the finish line. You are putting yourself out there and if you fail it is all down to you. Yes, you may have a slight illness or injury but you are the one who has made the decision to get to the start line and to compete, so it is you who is declaring that you are ready.

If you have ever been on the start line of a race and listened to other athletes you would think that none of them should be there. Everyone you talk to is either carrying an injury, just getting over an illness, has done too much/too little training or has not raced for ages. Why do we do this, it's simple, fear of failure. If I tell these stories then I will not be expected to do well and when I do it will be even more astounding. When was the last time any runner said to you at the start of an event, "I feel great and I'm going to smash my way to an incredible time today". The fear of failure is always there so the excuses are there to explain why you failed before you have. I have always tried to be honest with people before I run and have always declared my state of mind and fitness before the start. What's the point in telling everyone you are not really up for it when you know as soon as the gun goes you will off and running like your life depended upon it.

Running at the right pace is such an important part of successful racing, but running in the right direction is even more important. In road races this is not usually a problem but for off road events it becomes a major part of the race. Like the time I ran leg 7 of the Cotswold Way Relay for Bitton. The start was in Dursley and I was in the top ten by the time we reached North Nibley. There is then a steep climb up to the Tyndale Monument before you drop down into the woods about a mile and a half from the finish in Wotton-under-Edge. When we entered the woods I was in sixth place, by the time I came out the other side I was minutes away from missing the cut off time. My mistake was following other people going into the woods and not concentrating. After about five minutes in the woods the two runners in front of me stopped and asked me if I knew the way. We were lost and as I had been more concerned about keeping with them and did not have a clue where we were.

On another occasion on the first day of the LAMM in the Scottish Highlands the weather was particularly bad with low cloud and rain. I was running with Nick Thorpe and had the very important role of navigator, which was crucial in such conditions. Lots of good compass work and map reading saw us hit the first five checkpoints in good time. Then the cloud cleared just after checkpoint five and gave us good visibility. I looked at the map and at the terrain in front of us pointing out where we had to go next. I was now relying on visual and we ended up in the wrong valley which cost us about forty five minutes as well as the huge amount of energy that was needed to get us back on track. In those moments that slight loss of concentration was costly. Always know where you are on the map, check where you need to go and then check again before going too far. It is very easy when visibility is good to make the terrain fit the map and even when it is not quite right your brain can tell you that what you see is what is on the map. No matter how much you may think it is not quite right, the compass is never wrong and will always get you moving in the right direction.

Coaching and mentoring has always been something I enjoy doing, get me talking about running and you may never get me to stop. When Ira Rainey first approached me about his marathon aspirations I spent quite a bit of time talking to him about his previous marathons and how he had felt they had gone. He felt he was under achieving because he had not gone under four hours and felt this was not an unrealistic target. Looking at his training and racing I agreed with him.

Ira wanted a training plan but he did not want it to be too

regimented. He wanted flexibility and did not want a plan that dictated what he needed to do on each day of the week. So I gave him a sixteen week plan that basically said what his target mileage was for the week. Within that week he must do two quality sessions, one on the track and one other, either a 'Tempo' run or hill reps, and a long run. These three basic elements could be done on whatever day he wanted to do them but never on consecutive days. The remainder of the mileage could be done at any time of the week and as it increased I suggested twice a day runs. I told Ira that for the first few weeks he may struggle while his body adjusted to these new demands, but to stick with it and it would become more comfortable. The plan also had weeks when he had to run a race over a set distance, starting with 5k and building up to a half marathon four weeks before his marathon. We had regular discussions on how it was going throughout the sixteen weeks and I was monitoring his progress in races. When he started his three week taper we had more discussions and then about two weeks before his marathon I told him that his target was not four hours but three hours and forty five minutes. He was a bit shocked but I gave him his race plan and told him that if he stuck to this plan then he would get a great time. Ira had trained hard and had shown through his race times that he was easily capable of getting under four hours. He phoned me after his marathon, he had done three hours forty six minutes and fifty six seconds, this time was over twenty minutes faster than his previous best.

Ira was a case of someone who had the sub four hours in him, he just needed a little direction on how to achieve it. The marathon is a very unforgiving distance and if you get it slightly wrong then you will be punished for it. I knew this from my own experiences but had finally managed to build myself a marathon story which I would think about as I raced this particular distance. My belief is that if all the training had gone well and I had tapered as I should leading up to the event, then I would get to the start line feeling anxious but confident. I then find that for the first couple of miles my legs are a little tight due to doing less and less over the previous three weeks. At around five miles everything starts to fall into place as the stiffness disappears and my legs remember all the hard work I have done in training. I am totally relaxed running strong and feeling great. I think at this point a lot of people feel so good they push the pace and go quicker than the target pace. It is at the point you feel at your best when it is most important to maintain the target pace and go no quicker no matter how good you feel. This is because by half way it all starts to get more difficult. I find that the period between twelve and eighteen the most crucial part of the race. My focus is to just tick off the miles at the target pace, and this normally takes all my concentration and effort. If I am still maintaining target pace at eighteen it is usually taking every bit of effort and focus. It is then time to play the mind games. I promise myself that I will do just one more mile at this pace then I will slow down a bit. When I get to nineteen I do the same thing and then again after each mile. Before I know it I am at twenty two or twenty three and the finish is in sight. This has worked for me on so many occasions and, when it has, my split times have been pretty even. Most people I have mentored to better marathon times did so by following this simple process of making those mile times as even as possible. If your target time says eight minutes per mile then stick with that throughout, even when you feel you can go quicker.

28 6-LANGDALE TO BROCKHOLE

"I'll be happy if running and I can grow old together."
— Haruki Murakami

As I sat at a table in the Stickle Barn Tavern I was still finding it difficult to comprehend what had happened. I really felt I was going well over that last section. Feeling sorry for myself I sat alone, took off my rucksack, shoes and socks while helping myself to a plate of chips with loads of salt. I looked around me and more runners were coming into the Tavern, obviously they also had missed the cut off.

After about twenty minutes another runner came over to me and said "as it's going to be dark from here on in, would you like to run together for company?". "Sorry" I said "but I'm out, I missed the cut off". "how can that be?" he replied "you were here before me and I am still in the race, you are doing the one hundred kilometre aren't you?". "Yes" I replied. "well if that's the case you are still in because the cut off is midnight". I was stunned, then, it dawned on me that the marshal thought I was part of the fifty kilometre event because the runner who came in just before me was probably in the fifty. I immediately got up and walked barefoot over to the marshal who had spoken to me and said "excuse me but I came in about twenty minutes ago and you told me I had missed the cut off. I am doing the one hundred kilometre and have been told that the cut off is midnight"? "I'm so sorry" he said "I just assumed you were a fifty kilometre runner because you came in with the other guy who was in the fifty". Incredibly, I was still in the race. I stood there quite stunned for a while trying to get my head together and thinking about how I was going to get myself motivated to start running again. I went back to my table and said to the other runner "as long as you don't mind waiting ten minutes for me, I would like to set out with you". "Fine" he said "I will go and tell the others, there will be four of us running together".

My mind was in a spin, I had to put my shoes and socks back on and get my head torch out of my bag. It was also getting cooler so I would probably need another layer on.

The main issue was how to get myself going. As any runner will tell you, once an event is over you tend to switch off, both physically and mentally. Could I really get myself going again after taking a thirty minute break at the end of fifty miles and thirteen gruelling hours of tough unforgiving mountain terrain? There was only one way to find out. So fifteen minutes later the four of us stepped out of the Stickle Barn Tavern determined to complete the remaining twelve miles or so of this remarkable race.

We came out of the tavern crossed the road and picked up a decent level path. We were shuffling along and my legs were really struggling to move. The others were quite shocked at what I had been through at the last checkpoint. I was just relieved that they had spoken to me, otherwise I would still be sat there thinking my race was over. It was during this section that I realised my head torch was totally inadequate. I could hardly see the terrain before me, so I spent most of my time running behind the others using their light to see where I was going.

After a long run down towards Chapel Stile we finally cut left through the village and started to make our up towards Loughrigg Fell. My body was still in shutdown mode and I was finding it difficult to get any sort of running out of my legs. Luckily the others were very tired as well so I managed to keep up.

Up to now I always knew where I was, having walked and run in most areas of the Lake District, but on this section I completely lost my sense of direction and had no idea where I was or how far we still had to go. This was a combination of being very tired, running in the dark and following others rather than finding my own way. I was really grateful that I did not have find my way because I felt exhausted and am convinced I would have walked a great deal more if it wasn't for the others pulling me along. The thing that kept me going was the thought of trying to run with the tiny light source I had brought with me. It would have meant I would have been a lot slower covering the ground. As it was it took us over two hours to complete this six and a half mile section.

What a relief to reach Ambleside and the last checkpoint. Again I took on copious amounts of flat coke and steeled myself for the final four plus miles. I was more tired than I had ever felt before but I knew I was just a few miles from the finish. We set of from Ambleside and started the climb through the woods to High Skelghyll. It was during this section that we became a bit lost as there seemed to be a lack of directional arrows at path junctions. We carried on, not sure of where we were going, and after quite some time came upon a race marshal who was hanging out glow sticks as route markers. She told us that someone had been through the woods and removed all the glow stick markers and she was going back over the route and putting them back. Luckily we found out that we had not gone too far off course and from here on we would be okay because she had replaced them all. They had been alerted to the problem a little earlier when someone had seen runners using the road to get from Ambleside to Brockhole.

We continued on our way and I started to lag further behind the others. I told them to carry on and said I would meet them at the finish. One had already dropped off the pace and the other two were stronger than me so forged ahead. Suddenly I was on my own and really struggling. My head torch was all but useless so I could see nothing in front of me. I stumbled and tripped my way along until I finally reached the very rocky track that we had ascended at the beginning of the race. Buoyed by the fact that the finish was now in sight I started my way down the track. I could see no torch light in front of me and only one some distance behind me.

The lack of a good light source meant I had to walk this downward track, and I was cursing as I tripped and stumbled my way down. Only about a mile to go and here I was walking down a hill. Gradually the light behind me got closer and as he passed me I tried to hang on but my tired and aching body soon gave up and I was walking again. My head torch had now gone completely and again I cursed as I stumbled along the track. It was at this point I decided to ring Claire and see if she had finished. Thankfully she answered the phone and I told her to get to the end of the track and start walking up it with a torch so I could see where I was going.

After another five minutes of darkness I saw a light ahead of me. I met with Claire and took her torch and we set off down the track to the road. Suddenly I could see where I was going and managed to start running again. We reached the road and I crossed over to the Brockhole Centre. A short run down past the centre then back up to the finish banner. My bruised, battered and exhausted body finally crossed the finish line in a time of seventeen hours eighteen minutes and fifty one seconds. I was overjoyed at finishing if not a bit disappointed at the time it had taken me. I stumbled into the Brockhole Centre and sat down totally spent. For the next thirty minutes I could not move and felt physically sick. Claire said I went as white as a sheet and I could not even talk. I barely managed to speak to the guys who had helped me so much over the last two sections but even in the midst of this I felt such an overwhelming sense of satisfaction and achievement.

So it was done. A race I had gone into with so many negative thoughts, with an injury, I had had many moments of doubt, had fallen, had been told I was out and had always felt I probably would not finish. But not only had I finished I had come thirty eighth after being seventy fifth at checkpoint one. I was also second in my age group and after the event I found out that the head torch that had passed me down the last hill was the first veteran sixty. Thirty six runners had dropped out but I managed to carry on. After the event the route was re-calculated and the distance was adjusted to 112km, not the original 100km, so I had run even further than I initially thought. This race really showed me what could be achieved even when you felt it was impossible. The weather had been kind to us but it was still a huge undertaking. I drew so much from this race in terms of mental attitude. When I was told my race was over it would have been so much easier to go with that and then blame it on the organisers afterwards, but to be honest when the other athlete told me I was still in the race my only thought was how I could get myself motivated and going again. The thought of giving up and staying in the pub eating chips only entered my head very briefly before I cast it aside and got on with the task in front of me. Those last few miles were agonisingly slow as I stumbled about in the dark cursing my stupidity in choosing such a small head torch, and my legs had never been so tired. But once again I had showed that even when running on tired legs I still had the ability to keep moving forward toward the finish line.

Distance covered 61.4 miles
Time taken 17hrs 18mins 51secs
Overall position at Ambleside 40th
Overall position at Brockhole 38th

Printed in Great Britain
by Amazon